KITCHEN, VILLA BOSCOBEL

AMERICA'S
HISTORIC HOUSES
and RESTORATIONS
Irvin Haas

HAWTHORN BOOKS, INC. ★ *Publishers* ★ NEW YORK

First Edition, November, 1966

ACKNOWLEDGMENTS

The publisher and author gratefully acknowledge the following photographers and organizations whose interest, cooperation and permission to reproduce photographs have made possible the publication of this book:

Douglas Armsden, Edmund Barrett, Gene Baxter, Samuel Chamberlain, Jack Coleman, the Connecticut Historical Society, the Delaware State Archives, Clare H. Ebeling, A. Wilson Embrey III, Flournoy, Louis H. Frohman, Madlin Futrell, Sherman A. Gessert, Jr., the Hartford Courant, the Hughes Company, James N. Keen, Robert L. Knudsen, Long Beach News Bureau, Louis S. Mariel, Mellow, W. F. Miller & Co., the Milwaukee Journal, Eric H. Muller, National Trust for Historic Preservation, Robert L. Nay, North Carolina State Department of Archives and History, Woody Ogden, Perry Studio Photographers, Edward Ragland, Abbie Rowe, Savannah News-Press, Ed T. Simmons, Judson Smith, the Society for the Preservation of New England Antiquities, Sunday Republican Magazine, Gene Taggart, Taylor and Dull, Stephen M. Toth, Virginia Chamber of Commerce, Danny Wann, and the historic houses and restorations included in this book.

for Irene, Karin and Peter

CONTENTS

MIDDLE ATLANTIC

SOUTH

MIDWEST & WEST

FOREWORD

These are perilous times for the pitifully few historical landmarks remaining to us. In the countryside, as in towns and cities, historical buildings and sites are menaced today as never before. Each year our precious heritage of "living history" falls victim to abuse, neglect, and destruction. The enemies are poorly planned highway programs, exploding suburbs, urban blight, and the voracious demands for parking space. As one leading worker for preservation, Lewis Mumford, puts it, "Our national flower may yet be the cement cloverleaf."

Fortunately, the idea of historical preservation has been spreading. The tourist has joined with the historian to make an irresistible team that demands that key aspects of our past everywhere be preserved. This concern for preservation is not uniquely American. Europe, the Middle East, and the Far East have found their heritages fast disappearing due to the same blights that infect us. They too have aroused their governments to pass legislation to protect and preserve their historic buildings and sites.

Our own preservation movement began in New York State with the acquisition of Washington's Revolutionary Headquarters in Newburgh, Orange County, New York, in 1850. Nine years later Mount Vernon, Washington's home in Virginia, was purchased by the Mount Vernon Ladies Association, which continues to administer it. Since that time the preservation movement has advanced sporadically, mainly through the efforts of local organizations whose horizons were limited to the houses and sites of their own localities. A great broadening of the range and activity of preservation started with the incorporation of the National Council for Historic Sites and Buildings in 1947 and the founding of its successor, the National Trust for Historic Preservation in 1949. The Trust is a private organization with a membership of more than 540 affiliated preservation, patriotic, historical, and architectural societies whose dedicated purpose is "guarding America's heritage." Among these admirable, hard-working organizations are regional societies like the Society for the Preservation of New England Antiquities, which administers as many as fifty-seven historic houses, and the Association for the Preservation of Tennessee Antiquities, which maintains ten historic sites. The Colonial Dames of America is particularly active in the preservation movement; it owns or administers some forty-two historic houses. Maryland, Virginia, Delaware, Iowa, and North Carolina all have Societies for the Preservation of Antiquities. Seventy municipalities have adopted legislation protecting landmarks and historic districts. These are the enlightened efforts that are perpetuating the highest ideals of the preservation movement.

The United States government has recognized the importance of preservation. In the Historic Sites Act of 1935 Congress declared that "it is a national policy to preserve for public use historic sites, buildings, and objects of national significance for the inspiration and benefit of the people of the United States." The act directed the Secretary of the Interior to make a nationwide survey of historic sites for the purpose of determining which possess exceptional value. This directive led to the National Survey of Historic Sites and Buildings. Hundreds of exceptionally valuable sites were found during the National Survey. Many were already being preserved by state, local, and private agencies. But many others were endangered by decay or destruction.

Obviously the federal government could not acquire all significant sites. Only through the cooperation of federal, state and local groups, and individuals, could the American people hope to encompass the vast scope of historical conservation in the United States.

To solve this problem The Registry of National Historic Landmarks was founded in October, 1960. Its purpose is twofold: to recognize and encourage the continuation of preservation efforts being conducted by state, local, and private agencies, and to call attention to those sites of exceptional value that need to be preserved. So far, 548 buildings and sites have been declared eligible for the National Registry of Landmarks.

An excellent and increasingly popular method of maintaining and exhibiting historic houses is the creation of a restored village, either one that had actually existed or the invention of one for the purpose of presenting a central theme. These "living museums" consolidate preservation problems into a compact and easily managed area and have become very popular with the public. Sturbridge Village in Massachusetts, the Farmer's Museum at Cooperstown, New York, Greenfield Village at Dearborn, Michigan, Mystic Seaport in Connecticut, and the Shaker Community at Hancock, Massachusetts, are among those restorations or recreations that are having outstanding success.

This book is a tribute to the entire preservation movement in the United States. It is an inventory of their efforts. In deciding which historic houses and restorations were to be represented in this book, I was guided by the sensible criteria adopted by the Registry of National Historic Landmarks:

1. Structures or sites at which events occurred that have made an outstanding contribution to, are identified prominently with, or best represent the broad cultural, political, economic, military, or social history of the nation and from which visitors may grasp the larger patterns of our American heritage.

2. Structures or sites associated importantly with the lives of outstanding historic personages.

3. Structures or sites associated significantly with an important event that best represents some great ideal or idea of the American people.

4. Structures that embody the distinguishing characteristics of an architectural type specimen, exceptionally valuable for a study of a period style or method of construction; or a notable structure representing the work of a master builder, designer, or architect.

There are many historic houses that are cherished and preserved locally because they have associations with local history and personages of great interest to the community rather than to the state or nation. Reluctantly I have eliminated these, secure in the knowledge that they will continue to be visited, discussed and preserved by the proud community that harbors them.

I am grateful for the cooperation I have received from the curators and committees responsible for all of the houses and restorations listed. I am grateful to Colin Ritter, Acting Chief of Information of the National Park Service, U.S. Department of the Interior; to Mrs. Helen Duprey Bullock, Director of the Department of Information of the National Trust for Historic Preservation, and to Bertram Little, Director of the Society for the Preservation of New England Antiquities. They are only three of the many who have helped me compile this book.

IRVIN HAAS

ADAMS MANSION

ADAMS NATIONAL HISTORIC SITE
QUINCY, MASSACHUSETTS

The Adams National Historic Site is a living memorial to four generations of one family, a family that played a part in shaping the destiny of America. Distinguished in public life and in our national literature, men of each of these generations left their stamp on the history of the United States.

When not at the seat of government, John Adams, first Vice President of the United States and second President of the United States, lived at the Adams mansion. He was born on October 19, 1735, graduated from Harvard College in 1755, and admitted to the bar in 1758. He married Abigail Smith of Weymouth, Massachusetts, in 1764. She was the first mistress of the White House and the only woman in our history who has been the wife of one president and the mother of another. John Adams had a long and distinguished career; among his many posts were member of the Committee of Five to draft the Declaration of Independence, commissioner to France, minister plenipotentiary to Holland, envoy to the Court of St. James, Vice President during Washington's term, and President of the United States in 1796. He lived to see his son elected to the presidency and died on July 4, 1826.

John Quincy Adams was born in 1767. He gained an extraordinary knowledge of Europe because of his father's various foreign posts. He graduated from Harvard College in 1787. He was Minister to the Netherlands, and during his father's presidency he was Minister to Prussia. He was elected to the United States Senate in 1803. Under President Madison he became, in 1809, Minister to Russia. He signed the Treaty of Ghent, which ended the War of 1812. He was in Paris to witness Napoleon's triumphal return from Elba. Adams next went to England as Minister to the Court of St. James. In 1817

he became President Monroe's Secretary of State and was jointly responsible with the President for the promulgation of the Monroe Doctrine. In 1825 he became the sixth President of the United States. Retiring to Quincy in 1829, within two years he was elected to Congress, where he served continuously for seventeen years. He was the only President to become a member of the House of Representatives after a term in the White House. On February 21, 1848, at the age of eighty-one, he was stricken on the floor of the House, literally dying at his post.

Charles Francis Adams, son of the sixth President, was born August 18, 1807 Like his father before him, he traveled extensively in Europe from the age of two. He was graduated from Harvard College in 1825 and was admitted to the bar in 1829. He spent some weeks in the office of Daniel Webster. He married Abigail Brown of Boston in 1829. After serving in the Massachusetts Legislature, he was nominated for Vice President on Martin Van Buren's ticket in 1848. Elected to Congress in 1858 and again in 1860, he was chosen by Lincoln as Minister to the Court of St. James, where he served during the years of the Civil War. Resigning in 1868, he declined the presidency of Harvard University and retired to Quincy. He wrote on history for the *North American Review,* published the letters of his grandmother, Abigail Adams, *The Works of John Adams* in ten volumes, a biography of his grandfather and published his father's diary. He died on November 21, 1886.

Charles Francis Adams left four sons. The eldest was John Quincy, who served on Governor Andrew's staff during the Civil War. Charles Francis Adams Jr. served in the Union Army throughout the Civil War and rose to the rank of Colonel. He was mustered out in 1865 with the brevet of Brigadier General. In 1884 he became president of the Union Pacific Railroad. He was the author of a number of books on historical subjects.

Henry Adams, like his forebears, graduated from Harvard College, studied civil law in Berlin, and then began his travels, which carried him about the world for many years. He served as his father's secretary in Washington during 1860–61 and accompanied him to London. Returning in 1868, he taught history at Harvard for seven years and edited the *North American Review*. He was the author of biographies of Albert Gallatin, John Randolph, and George Cabot Lodge; two novels; the History of the United States from 1800 to 1817 in nine volumes; *Mount-Saint Michel and Chartres;* and the American classic, *The Education of Henry Adams*. He died in 1918.

Brooks Adams graduated from Harvard College in 1870. He too served as his father's secretary and as a member of the Massachusetts Constitutional Convention of 1917. He was the last of his family to occupy the Adams Mansion at Quincy. He wrote a number of books on economic and historical subjects. He died in 1927.

The Adams Mansion was first named *Peacefield* by John Adams. The oldest part of the house was built in 1731 by Major Leonard Vassall, a wealthy West Indian sugar planter. The house then consisted only of the paneled room, west entry, dining room on the ground floor, and two bedrooms on the second floor, and three smaller rooms in the attic. The kitchen and servants' quarters were not attached to the house. John Adams bought the house from Major Vassall's grandson and took possession in 1788. During his presidency he built the large gabled ell containing the long room, east entry, and upstairs study. In 1836 John Quincy Adams added the passage along the north side of the house connecting the two ells. In 1869 Charles Francis Adams added thirty feet to the kitchen ell for servants' quarters; the following year he built the stone library overlooking his grandmother's garden and in 1873 the stone stable. The present entrance gates were added by Brooks Adams in 1906.

After his retirement from the presidency in 1801, John Adams lived in the house until his death in 1826. John Quincy Adams and Charles Francis Adams made it their summer home, and many summers were spent there by both Henry and Brooks Adams. Much of the furniture within the house reflects the diplomatic backgrounds of the Adams as each came back with prized possessions from their various European missions.

The continuity of life in the house is best shown by the furnishings, as the various objects are of successive periods—each generation contributed something of itself. The house is not a "period piece" but a house that clearly shows the ever-changing style and taste of its occupants from 1788 to 1927.

The ADAMS NATIONAL HISTORIC SITE is on Adams Street, Newport Avenue, and Furnace Brook Parkway, Quincy, Massachusetts, about eight miles south of Boston. It is on State Route 135 and adjacent to State Route 3. It may be visited from 9:00 A.M. to 5:00 P.M. every day from April 19 to November 10. There is "a nominal admission fee," which is waived for children under twelve years of age.

WATERTOWN, MASSACHUSETTS

Reclaimed from near ruin and carefully restored in 1923 by William Sumner Appleton, the Abraham Browne House is an excellent example of seventeenth-century architecture. Part of its charm lies in the fact that it has remained for many years in the family of the original settler, Captain Abraham Browne. He gave the house to his son Samuel in 1729. Samuel gave it to his nephew Jonathan B. Jr., who gave it to his son Adam and to Francis. Thus the house was kept in the family until 1897.

The house is Gothic in construction and appearance, with its steeply pitched roof. The present pilastered chimney was a conjectural feature of the restoration. The form of the original chimney is not known. The pilastered chimneys of early New England houses are striking examples of our architectural continuity. They also refute the notion that the Puritans rejected every bit of ornamentation.

The Abraham Browne House has one of the few original three-part casement-window frames known to exist in New England. During its restoration it was discovered that a three-part casement window in the North Hall of the original house had been left there when the original eighteenth-century addition was made. This frame was the first to be discovered in a New England house.

The interior is distinguished by an enormous fireplace spanned by one massive lintel of oak. The wall sheathing is of flat white pine boards laid horizontally, oiled and waxed, and weathered a toast brown. The floor boards are of wide and durable white pine. The ceiling is a sturdy network of hewn oak beams.

The ABRAHAM BROWNE HOUSE is located at 562 Main Street in Watertown, Massachusetts. It is open every day except Saturday from 2:00 P.M. to 5:00 P.M. from May through October and November through April. The admission charge is twenty-five cents.

ABRAHAM BROWNE HOUSE

CAMBRIDGE, MASSACHUSETTS

The Cooper-Frost-Austin House is unique in a way that could not have been foreseen when it was built in 1657. At that time Linnaean Street was but a grassy way, which came to be called "Love Lane"; the Common, where citizens pastured their cows, extended from Harvard Square up to the house's front door; behind the house a garden sloped upward to Gallows Hill. The Cooper-Frost-Austin House is not only the oldest house in Cambridge but also exemplifies the kind of modest homestead that seldom received the care and attention needed to maintain it for centuries. This house was lucky, however, because it remained in the hands of the same family from the time of its construction until its sale in 1912 to the Society for the Preservation of New England Antiquities.

Linnaean Street today is an area thickly settled with houses and the Radcliffe College dormitories; the site of the gallows has long disappeared under brick apartment buildings and large homes. The Common, now a public park, has shrunk to less than a third of its original size and is separated from the Cooper-Frost-Austin House by blocks of buildings; but in 1912 the Director of the Society talked to elderly residents of the area who could remember standing at the front door and looking down all the way to Harvard Square.

A romantic story is included in the annals of the family who occupied the house for 255 years. After the death of Walter Cooper III his widow married Jonathan Hill. Two children were born in the house of that marriage, Jonathan Cooper Hill in 1763 and Lydia in 1766. When Lydia was baptized in the Meetinghouse in the College Yard, there was present a student, Jeremiah Fogg, of Kensington, New Hampshire, who vowed that he would marry little Lydia. The Revolutionary War broke out when she was ten years old, and Major Jeremiah Fogg came to Cambridge with his New Hampshire men and renewed acquaintance with Lydia; and

when she was old enough, he did indeed marry her. Outside the west parlor of the house the red lilac Lydia Hill planted in 1775 still blooms in the spring.

Nestled among its grove of saplings, the Cooper-Frost-Austin House captures in a nutshell the town that used to be. Painted white, of modest size, it is an old farmhouse complete with connected sheds. The steeply pitched gable roof, the pilastered brick chimney, the overhang of the east gable, and the leanto in the rear demonstrate its seventeenth-century construction. Its original thick oak beams still support it, and most of the old wooden clapboards, fastened with hand-wrought nails, are still intact.

The interior has been restored to present an authentic home of the period. The ceilings are low, the atmosphere simple and cosy. Much original material was discovered under layers of what later inhabitants considered fashionable additions; for example, the fireplace in the east parlor, which is now in its original form, had had not only a second fireplace built within and over it but also a third. One of the bedrooms on the second floor shows some fine old sheathing, and the other has interesting paneling. Around the central chimney are grouped several large fireplaces, each with a large beam across the top. Some of its later features of the eighteenth and nineteenth centuries have been retained, so that as a whole the house offers a bit of a survey of domestic architectural history.

The COOPER-FROST-AUSTIN HOUSE is located at 21 Linnaean Street in Cambridge, Massachusetts. It is off Massachusetts Avenue, north of Harvard Square. It is open Monday and Thursday from 2:00 P.M. to 5:00 P.M. and on Tuesday from 7:00 P.M. to 9:00 P.M. from June through October. From November through May it is open on Thursday from 2:00 P.M. to 5:00 P.M. and on Tuesday from 7:00 P.M. to 9:00 P.M. The admission charge is twenty-five cents.

COOPER-FROST-AUSTIN HOUSE

SAMUEL FOWLER HOUSE

DANVERSPORT, MASSACHUSETTS

Seven hundred and seventy dollars is the sum accounted by Samuel Fowler for building his square brick house in 1810. As a postscript to his account he wrote, "On the 29 Day of October I moved in my brick house with a wife and 5 children and 12 in femely." Samuel Fowler himself was a rather exceptional man. Educated at the simple village school, he went on to use his training and to further his abilities. The dozen existing ledgers of his bookkeeping system attest to the effectiveness with which he had studied. In 1799 he bought the land on which the house stands and began to invest in mills and to add to his real-estate holdings. He was the first to start the tanning industry in this part of Danvers, and with seven others he shared the cost of building the Liberty Bridge.

Fowler's life was one of temperance, generosity, and perseverance. He was always willing to help financially in projects that tended to improve the village and town. He regularly attended the Unitarian meetinghouse in North Beverly. He rose regularly at four in the morning, winter and summer, and went to his mills to superintend the beginning of the day's work. He enjoyed his apiary and orchard garden and raised an abundance of peaches—and often sent one of the boys with a cartload to Marblehead to barter for codfish.

The house itself is sober and simple. The only ornamentation on the exterior is the fanlight over the door, the plain rows of sidelights, horizontal carving in the cornice, and the ivy that climbs along the walls. Its beauty comes from the balanced proportions of the windows and doors cut into the firm brick walls.

The interior displays a similar restraint. In the parlor, for instance, the mantel, pedestal, and cornice are carved very delicately but not extravagantly. "Egg and dart" and "scroll" carvings ornament the front hall. Throughout the house various motifs, reedings, and flutings decorate the woodwork and emphasize the harmonious proportions of the elements. The house contains several interesting wallpapers. In the front entry, applied in nineteen-inch squares, is one that Nancy McClelland in her book, *Historic Wallpapers,* describes as "Pompeian Medallion made by Asa Smith of Baltimore who had a factory between 1800 and 1810 . . . his most distinguished design." The walls of the southwest parlor are covered with a modern print that uses the original old blocks for the famous scenic paper "Roman Chase," designed by Jean Zuber in 1838.

The house came to the Society for the Preservation of New England Antiquities in 1912. The Misses Adelaide and Sarah Putnam Fowler, who continued to inhabit it after its sale, ran a little shop in the front parlor, where they sold laces, bobbins, thread, tapes and similar items, until their deaths in the 1930s.

The SAMUEL FOWLER HOUSE is located at 166 High Street in Danversport, Massachusetts. Turn right at exit 15 on Route 128. It is open Monday, Wednesday, and Thursday from 2:00 P.M. to 5:00 P.M. from mid-April to mid-September. The admission charge is twenty-five cents.

HAMILTON HOUSE

SOUTH BERWICK, MAINE

Colonel Jonathan Hamilton became rich through retail trade "selling salt-fish, molasses, rum, sugar and tea to farmers in exchange for wood, timber, poultry, butter and eggs." He resolved to build the finest house in Berwick. It was in 1788 that his mansion on the high bluff jutting out into the Quamphegan was completed.

Colonel Hamilton built this fine house at a time when Maine shipping fortunes were recovering from the low state occasioned by the Revolution and his trade with the West Indies had again resumed. He had come into his own as a leading citizen of Old Berwick at about the time of moving into his mansion. From the windows of the stately drawing room he watched his own ships come around the bend. To the north and east lay the stables and office buildings, slave quarters, spinning house and high green fields.

In 1800 his wife Mary died. He married a widow, Charlotte Swett soon after. Then in the autumn of 1802, Colonel Hamilton died. He left no will, and hard days were ahead for his estate. His wife moved to Exeter. His daughter Olive and her husband Joshua Haven moved into the mansion, but the divided fortune of the family rapidly disintegrated, and their residence in the mansion was short.

The mansion and its grounds changed hands several times, and it physically declined until it reached the point of decay. In 1839 Alpheus and Betsey Goodwin bought the great gray house. They tore down neglected warehouses, pastured sheep on the sloping green, and replaced the formal garden with an apple orchard. Alpheus Goodwin had a fine appreciation for the old house, and so did his descendants. For well over half a century the Goodwins maintained their mansion without making a single structural change. In 1898 Emily Tyson bought the Hamilton House and its 110 acres. She made the first structural change in the history of the mansion. A stairway leading from the east door was removed, extending the length of the dining room, and two small latticed wings were built at the sides. A door was cut into the north parlor to give the house four entrances. In 1949 Mrs. Henry G. Vaughan, daughter of Emily Tyson, bequeathed the mansion to the Society for the Preservation of New England Antiquities. They restored it to its original nearly four-square proportions.

Visitors are impressed by the terraced lawns rising steeply from the river on two sides, windows graduating from eighteen lights on the first floor to fifteen and finally to twelve, the steeply pitched roof, and four massive chimneys reaching far above.

Doors open on three sides: to the southern riverside, to the service court on the east, and to the carriage entrance on the north. Decoration is not excessive. The restrained rhythm of the dormers, which project with balanced triangular and broken arch pediments, a simple cornice below the roof, two fine Palladian windows, and beaded pilasters on the front entrance, provide the only ornamentation other than the subtle rectangular shape of the clapboarded house itself.

On entering one is impressed by the soft faded walls in the capacious hall, which broadly bisects two stories. The original paper with its classic Greco-Roman arches has been reproduced. Handsome ship models are hung at each side. The Drawing Room to the left is a room of great dignity, with deep window seats and carved arches. Tall paneled shutters fold into reveals, and large brass box locks glisten on the doors. The floor is scattered with Oriental rugs, and there are wing chairs of considerable age. Two Chippendales flank a Sheraton ottoman, and there is a set of Hepplewhite chairs that was among the first cargo to come from England to Philadelphia after the War of 1812. The stark paneling of the chimney breast is relieved by a black basalt Wedgwood bust of Washington. Before the fireplace stand two fine mahogany pole screens. Through a doorway one glimpses a black and gold lacquered desk in the north parlor, a high mahogany breakfront, lacquered tables, candlestands, and a settee.

In the dining room the walls are painted in an appropriate classical theme of soft greens and blues. There is a handsome Hepplewhite inlaid sideboard of about the period of the house, with Chippendale trays and rare chestnut urns. An Adam filigree mirror and an 1800 Aaron Willard Jr. clock are on the walls. The mahogany table is graced by an unusual arrangement of crystal Waterford and dolphin Sandwich candlesticks.

In back of the Dining Room is the kitchen, with its vast fireplace and brick oven and ancient utensils for cooking. The spacious chambers above are rich with Bristol and Sandwich glass, early chairs, highboys and lowboys, field bedsteads and primitive hooked rugs, dolls and toys, and a connoisseur's collection of early prints, silhouettes, and paintings. It is little wonder that the American novelist Sarah Jewett chose the Hamilton House as a romantic setting for her novel, *The Tory Lover*.

The HAMILTON HOUSE is located in South Berwick, Maine. It can be reached by Route 236 from Portsmouth. Turn left off Route 236 eleven miles from Portsmouth opposite the junction with Route 91 from York. It is open Wednesday through Saturday from 1:00 P.M. to 5:00 from mid-June to mid-September. The admission charge is fifty cents.

HANCOCK SHAKER VILLAGE

VIEW FROM WEST LAUNDRY

22

HANCOCK, MASSACHUSETTS

The religious sect that became known as the Shakers began in England about 1706. In 1758 a twenty-two-year-old woman from Manchester, Ann Lee, joined the sect and became the most important of the movement's leaders. With eight followers, Mother Ann traveled to America in 1774. At Watervliet, New York, she organized the first of eighteen Shaker communities.

The major significance of the Shakers is that they formed the most successful communal so-ciety ever developed in America. They built their social and economic system on the early American culture, perfected it in some areas, and made numerous minor improvements. There are today only two communities of Shakers, one at Canterbury, New Hampshire, the other at Sabbathday Lake, Maine, with a total of twenty-two members.

In the early days the Shakers acquired large tracts of land and were highly successful farm-ers. They put several products on the market. Large-scale production was a natural outgrowth

of their mode of life, partly due to the large communal families, which necessitated the production and preservation of food and other supplies on a large scale. Their industry included the production of clothes, cloth, rugs, and chairs. Shaker furniture is eagerly sought after by antique collectors today. Their economic system was based on a combination of intensive agriculture, manufacture, and trade, and they were early leaders in certain phases of mass production in America.

The Shaker community at Hancock was formed in 1780, four years before Mother Ann died, and continued to prosper for over a century. At its peak before the Civil War the settlement had over 300 brethren and sisters, and its land holdings came to 2,000 acres. When in 1960 there were only three surviving members of the community, the property was offered for sale. A group of Massachusetts residents, architectural historians, scholars, and lovers of antiquities organized a nonprofit corporation, *Shaker Community, Inc.* to preserve for the public the cultural, historical, and architectural heritage of the Hancock Shakers; it bought the settlement's seventeen extant buildings and its remaining 932 acres of beautiful unspoiled pastures and woodland directly from the ministry of the Shakers, whose official designation is "The United Society of Believers in Christ's First and Second Appearing."

Restoration of buildings and land, with funds donated by individuals, business firms, and foundations, was begun in 1960. The buildings include a garden house with its herb garden designed from inspirational drawings. The guided tour starts there and continues to the Reception Center, where information on all Shaker matters can be had. A bookstore and an exhibition of inspirational drawings can also be seen. The 1830 brick dwelling, where once lived one hundred Believers, has twelve furnished rooms: gathering room (world's parlor), sister's waiting room, meeting room, trustee's office, ministry dining room, communal dining room, kitchen, school room, deaconess's sewing room, nurse shop, sisters' retiring room, one room of costumes, and two rooms showing architectural features of this and other Shaker communities. The Charles Sheeler Collection of furniture is in the meeting room, and there are public rest rooms.

The next building in the tour is the Brethren Shop, where the crafts of the Shakers can be seen—broommaking, chairmaking, carpentry,

cobbling, clockmaking, tinware, and tools. In the Sisters Shop food preserving, medicinal garden seeds, tailoring, spinning, and weaving can be seen. There are weaving demonstrations on the second floor. The Ministry Wash House has an early version of the Shaker stove. Hancock's most famous landmark, the Round Barn, was built in 1826 (the superstructure was rebuilt after a fire in 1864). The noted round stone barn was used for hay storage and fifty-two head of cattle. This is the Village's major restoration project. The visitor should note the unusual split chestnut beams and display of early sleighs.

The Laundry and Machine Shop were begun in 1790. The Laundry has a wash room, ironing room (with an unusual stove for heating irons), and a drying room. The machine shop is being restored. Basketmaking is demonstrated in the building. Across the street is the Meeting House, built in 1793 and moved to Hancock 122 miles across the state from a former Shaker community at Shirley, Massachusetts. There are the living quarters for Elders and Eldresses on the second floor. Concerts of Shaker music are given in this building. In the Ministry Shop the Elder's workroom is being restored. There is a further building, the Tan House, but the interior is not restored.

Hancock Shaker Village has an impressive educational program. In addition to its guided tour of the Village, it provides lecturers to groups, publishes material on Shaker history, crafts, architecture, art and music, and offers special exhibitions that interpret Shaker life by using both the fine permanent collection of furniture and artifacts belonging to the Village and many items on loan.

The VILLAGE is on U.S. Route 20, five miles west of Pittsfield, Massachusetts. It is approximately 150 miles from both Boston and New York and is reached easily from both the Massachusetts Turnpike and the Berkshire Spur of the New York State Thruway. It is open every day from 9:30 A.M. to 5:00 P.M., June 1 to October 15. Adults are admitted for $1.00 and children under twelve for fifty cents.

25

HARTFORD, CONNECTICUT

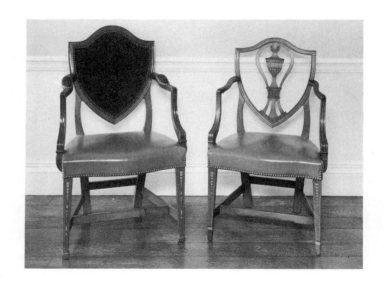

On May 26, 1790, the citizens of Hartford petitioned their Legislature for a new State House. The old house had, among other defects, a "lack of adequate ventilation in the existing structure that produces a general Langour of the spirits . . . and the lack of seats for the members in the Legislature caused pain and mortification." The petitioners submitted a suggested plan for a new State House showing a two-story brick building with round-topped windows. Written evidence suggests that the new State House was designed by Charles Bulfinch.

It took two years to get positive action on the matter. To finance its cost a lottery was proposed. This, though, was almost a complete failure. Other attempts were made but also failed. Finally, money was raised and in 1792 the State House Committee chose John Leffingwell to be the master builder. He did not delay, for on December 24, 1792, his subcontractors began to quarry stone, and in July of 1793 the cellar walls were started. The work proceeded without serious interruption, and on June 4, 1796, the Treasurer and Comptroller were authorized to take possession of their offices in the new State House. In that year the State House became the seat of government for Connecticut in Hartford.

From bills and other sources we can get a fairly good picture of how the State House was equipped and used. On the first floor we find the County Court. There the judge presided from a semicircular dais set against the north wall. Nearby a narrow stairway led to a retiring room in the basement for the jury. Across the open arcade were the offices of the comptroller, on the east, and the treasurer on the west. The office of the governor was in the southeast corner. The furniture there today is not the original equipment, but all is historic. The desk with bookcase belonged to Thomas Seymour, the first mayor of Hartford, and the high-backed corner chair belonged to Governor William Pitkin of East Hartford. The tall clock is also a Seymour piece. The treasurer's office is furnished with old-fashioned desks such as bookkeepers of the period would have used. The two armchairs belonged to prominent citizens, one to Roger Sherman, a signer of the Declaration of Independence, and the other to John Lawrence, treasurer of the state from 1769 to 1789.

On the west side of the second floor was the office of the secretary of the state. It bears no resemblance today to the simple business office it must have been. The north wing of the second floor was the Chamber of the House of Representatives. There the speaker presided from a platform at the center of the north wall, facing an aisle. On either side, facing this aisle, the representatives sat on settees painted green. Windsor chairs furnished additional seating.

The crowning glory of the State House is the Council, or Senate, Chamber. It occupies the south wing on the second floor. Its perfect proportions and simple architectural details are probably responsible for the preservation of the building. While much of the structure has been changed in various ways to meet the needs of later occupants, this room remains the same today as it did in 1796. Many of the original senate chairs were missing when restoration began, but collectors have made them available. The original layout of the Chamber has been duplicated. The semicircular desk for eighteen members dominates the layout, and the other pieces take the places they previously occupied in the legislative hall.

During the long history of the State House there have been interior and exterior changes. To the exterior were added a balustrade around the roof and a cupola. The cupola contains a statue of Justice on top and a clock.

On January 1, 1921, the people of Hartford were invited to the dedication of the restored building. In 1959 it was decided that while the City of Hartford would own the building, The Connecticut Historical Society would operate it as an historic site. In 1961 it was designated an historic landmark by the United States Department of the Interior.

ASSORTMENT OF CHINA, HARTFORD STATE HOUSE

*The STATE HOUSE is located at 800 Main
Street in Hartford, facing the Connecticut River,
Founder's Bridge and Constitution Plaza. It is
open from Tuesday to Saturday from 12:00
noon to 4:00 P.M. The adult admission charge
is fifty cents, children ten cents.*

SENATE CHAMBER, HARTFORD STATE HOUSE

NORTHEAST CHAMBER FIREPLACE, STEVENS HOUSE

WETHERSFIELD, CONNECTICUT

Isaac Stevens built this handsome village house in 1788–89 for his young bride. Today it remains charming, well proportioned, and substantial. The Connecticut Society of Colonial Dames in America purchased the house after it had been in the Stevens family for 175 years and restored it to its original state in structure, design, and colors, furnishing it with period pieces—in many cases with the Stevens family pieces.

Notable exterior features are the peaked roof and distinctive crown molding and the old red weatherboarding used on the rear elevation, which contrasts so pleasantly with the bayberry-green clapboards. The rear dooryard garden contains a bricked-in herb and flower garden, well house, grape arbor, and wood pile.

The dark green parlor opening off the central hall to the right has its dentil carving and fireplace mantel superimposed over earlier woodwork dating from about 1810. The room houses a rare Clementi piano, a Stevens family tip-tilt table displaying a pink and white Spode tea set, a handsome wing chair (1740–80) upholstered in deep red, and a fine Pembroke table.

The dark green dining room houses a Queen Anne table from the Stevens family, Queen Anne chairs, an Eli Terry clock, and other family pieces. The kitchen has been restored as a real working room with a wealth of wooden utensils, baskets, and the like that the Stevens' used. There are excellent examples of American pewter. The brick bakeoven is in its original state. The family room across from the kitchen has a delightful ladies' bonnet collection and an interesting folding bed. All these ground floor rooms are paneled, have fireplaces, sliding blinds, and contain much of the original hardware and floor boards.

Upstairs there are five bedrooms, the northeast chamber being the only exception to the house color scheme of tones of green. There the paneled fireplace wall is a deep green-blue with brick-red baseboards and fireplace facing.

An enchanting collection of children's books and toys is displayed in the small central bedroom; the tester bed in the southeast chamber is furnished with hangings reproduced from the original Stevens chintz, while other bedrooms are furnished with many Stevens pieces.

THE ISAAC STEVENS HOUSE

KITCHEN, STEVENS HOUSE

The ISAAC STEVENS HOUSE *is located at
215 Main Street in Wethersfield, Connecticut. It
is open to the public during the summer months
from 12:00 noon to 4:00 P.M. on Tuesday,
Thursday, and Friday. Adult admission is fifty
cents, children ten cents.*

THE GOVERNOR
JOHN LANGDON MANSION

PORTSMOUTH, NEW HAMPSHIRE

This is one of the fine Georgian houses in America. It was built by John Langdon, revolutionary leader, governor of New Hampshire, first president of the United States Senate, Acting President of the United States prior to the election of George Washington, and the first to notify Washington of his election to the presidency.

The Mansion has an elaborate entrance to the captain's walk, of Chippendale style, which crowns its hipped roof. Corinthian pilasters decorate corners of the facade, and delicate pillars of the same order uphold the balcony that tops the paneled front door. Three dormer windows ornamented with Georgian scrolls add to the beauty of the house.

The main stairway is imposing with balusters of three distinct designs to each tread. The newel post is carved from one piece of wood with its central spiral encased in four spindles of more simple design.

Among the furnishings are some pieces that belonged to the Langdon family. In the small south parlor or drawing room the original scenic paper of classical design is on the wall. The mantel and fire frame are intricately carved with leaves, vines, fruits, and flowers—the work of ship's carvers. The reception room or north parlor has a great chimney piece heavily carved and enhanced by graceful arches over windows on either side. The keystones of these arches are embellished with the fleur-de-lis (symbol of the visit of Louis Philippe, later King of France, in 1798.) This room is said to be half the size of the east room of the White House. The spinet and a portrait of Governor Langdon by Edward Savage are in this room.

The library is done in the Victorian manner with a bay window showing the Grecian influence. The card table belonged to Queen Victoria's father, the Duke of Kent. It was presented by the Duke to Governor William Eustis of Massachusetts, who married Caroline Langdon, niece of the governor. A wing was added in 1906, faithfully reproducing the architecture and style of the original house. The dining room is in this wing. It has four corner cupboards filled with rare china, including a gold band set used by the Langdons when they entertained President Washington in 1789.

The GOVERNOR JOHN LANGDON MANSION is located at 143 Pleasant Street in Portsmouth, New Hampshire. It is open weekdays from 1:00 P.M. to 5:00 P.M. from June 1 to mid-October. The admission charge is fifty cents.

MARBLEHEAD, MASSACHUSETTS

Colonel Jeremiah Lee built better than he knew when he erected his beautiful mansion in the heart of town in 1768. His handsome house stands today as a monument to the prosperity that was Marblehead's on the eve of the American Revolution.

Colonel Lee, one of the great merchants of his day, owned a fleet of ships that carried cured fish to the West Indies, the Wine Islands, Portugal, and Spain. On their return his vessels came laden with Cádiz salt, Madeira and Canary wine, Bilboa iron, pieces-of-eight, and West Indies molasses and sugar.

Colonel Lee served on the Committee of Safety with John Hancock in 1774–75. Through the door of his banquet hall came many men whose names are pages of American history— Washington, Lafayette, Monroe, and Jackson.

Unfortunately Jeremiah Lee did not enjoy his home for long. Even as the finishing touches were being put on the mansion questions such as Parliament's unlimited right to legislate for the colonies, the presence of British standing armies in America, and the despised tax on tea were being debated up and down the land. Marblehead merchants joined the economic boycott against English goods in 1769, and Jeremiah Lee served on the Watchdog Committee of Inspection that enforced compliance in 1770. Events that rocked the Massachusetts Bay colony —the Boston Massacre, Boston Tea Party, and Boston Port Bill—drove Lee even further into the camp of Marblehead's political radicals. He served as moderator at many a town meeting denouncing British acts. He was nominated to represent Marblehead at the Continental Congress in 1774 but declined the honor. The title "Colonel" stemmed from the commission he held in the Massachusetts militia in the 1750s.

Militarily, Lee's destiny was not on the battlefield but as a kind of quartermaster for the Massachusetts Minute Men. Serving on the famous Committee of Safety, he helped smuggle munitions and supplies into the colony. His duties on the Committee led indirectly to his death. When the British learned that the patriots had military supplies in Concord, a force of eight hundred Redcoats set out for Concord to seize the ammunition on April 18, 1775. That same evening Lee and Committee members Elbridge Gerry and Azor Orne were spending the night at Weatherby's Black Horse Tavern

on the road to Concord. When they heard the approaching column of Redcoats, they dashed out in their sleeping garments to hide in a field nearby. When the column moved on, the three men returned to recover their clothes. Tradition has it that Lee contracted a fatal illness from this exposure and died within three weeks of his narrow escape.

After the Colonel's death Martha Lee continued to live at the mansion. President Washington, President Monroe, and Andrew Jackson were all entertained there. In the final settlement of the Lee estate the mansion came into the possession of Chief Justice Samuel Sewall. When Sewall sold the house in 1804, it became a bank and was used as such for more than one hundred years. In 1909 the Lee Mansion passed into the hands of the Marblehead Historical Society.

Inspired by English Georgian style and fashioned along the lines of a great London town house, the mansion remains one of the finest examples of New England colonial architecture. Massive in scale and splendid in style, it was reputed to have cost its owner £10,000. Considering its three stories, its lofty cupola flanked by two massive chimneys, and its sixteen large rooms, this figure does not seem unreasonable. Mounting the steps of the pillared portico, the huge ten-paneled door swings open to reveal a front hall extending the full depth of the house. The hall has rich mahogany wainscoting and a stately staircase and is lighted by a great arch window on the stair landing. To the right is the dining room, with paneled wainscoting and fireplace wall with Corinthian pilasters. Little of Lee's furniture remains, but this room, like the others on the first two floors, is furnished with fittings that reflect the taste of the period. The fireplace is faced with tiles signed by the English craftsmen John Sadler.

Across the hall is the state dining room or banquet hall, where receptions were held on important occasions. There are two portraits of Colonel Lee and his wife, Martha, painted by John Singleton Copley in 1769. They are copies of the originals hanging in the Hartford Atheneum. The ceiling is composed of a combination of crushed oyster and clam shells held together by a binder. The sweeping staircase to the rear of the hall is seven feet wide and made of solid Santo Domingo mahogany.

CHIMNEYPIECE, DINING ROOM, LEE MANSION

The upper hall has splendid Queen Anne and Chippendale chairs, and across the hall is a perfect example of an eighteenth-century drawing room. Its paneled wainscoting, mantelpiece, and fireplace, done in the familiar egg and dart design, and Piranesi-like scenes on the wall paper speak of a life reminiscent of our own. Each of the rooms on the third floor has some highlight of special interest: a four poster, dolls, doll furniture, china and American primitives. From the glassed-in cupola there is a magnificent view of Massachusetts Bay. The master bedroom and especially the kitchen, with its fascinating collection of candle molds, mortars, pestles, rolling pins and nutmeg graters are quite charming. Colonel Lee's business office was in the counting room, where his private safe was built into the chimney and concealed behind a wall panel.

CENTER HALL, LEE MANSION

DINING ROOM, LEE MANSION

The LEE MANSION is located at 161 Washington Street in Marblehead, Massachusetts. It is also the home of the Marblehead Historical Society. It is open Monday through Saturday from 9:30 A.M. to 4:00 P.M. from May 18 to October 12. Admission is fifty cents.

THE GREAT ROOM, LEE MANSION

LEFFINGWELL INN

NORWICH, CONNECTICUT

One of the original settlers of Norwich in 1659 was William Backus Sr. His home lot descended to a son, Stephen. In 1675 he built a house; in 1700 he sold it to Ensign Thomas Leffingwell, who in 1701 was granted license to "keep a publique house of entertainment for strangers." It soon became necessary to enlarge the house, and the present hall and Great South Parlor with corresponding areas above and below were added. The Leffingwell family grew in numbers, importance, and resources, so about 1760 Christopher Leffingwell, the owner at that time, added the area containing the east hall, the George Washington Parlor, and the kitchen.

Norwich was a thriving community, being one of the twelve largest cities in the entire thirteen colonies in 1776. It was a center of vigorous support of the move for independence. There was no more ardent patriot than Christopher Leffingwell. By 1770 he had established the first paper mill in Connecticut, a stocking factory, pottery, chocolate mill, fulling mill, clothier's shop, and dye house. He was admirably fitted to become one of the most dependable sources of supply for the Continental Army, and in this respect General Washington relied heavily on him, as he did on Governor Jonathan Trumbull in nearby Lebanon. Leffingwell was also a constant advisor to Governor Trumbull and to Silas Deane. In 1775 he was appointed one of the Committee of Correspondence, and the news of the battles of Lexington and Concord reached the Norwich area through reports made to him.

PORRINGER AND SUGAR URN, LEFFINGWELL INN

The Tavern Room in the Inn, with its heavily shuttered windows insuring privacy, was the scene of many Revolutionary War conferences.

In the restoration the 1675 bedroom has been faithfully restored and furnished in the 1675 manner. A tavern room was also a part of the original house, but in the restoration the paneling of its four walls has been retained. This had been added by Christopher Leffingwell about 1760, but the original corner posts, beams, and wainscoting are clearly to be seen inside the paneled cupboards.

The Inn is unique in illustrating the development from seventeenth-century beginnings, simple, sturdy, concentrating on the essentials of existence, to a mid-eighteenth-century town house of an important and prosperous man of affairs who appreciated the finer things of life and could afford to have them. The Inn is furnished in large part with furniture and accessories that belonged in Norwich, so it truly reflects the life of our Norwich ancestors. Colonial New England is reflected with charm and fidelity. Mr. Henry F. DuPont (Winterthur Museum), chairman of Mrs. Kennedy's White House Committee, characterized the Inn: "It is the last word in restoration, so beautifully presented and full of interest."

LEFFINGWELL INN is easy to find from the Connecticut Turnpike. Follow Exit 81 East to the traffic light at its end. At the left is the Inn. During the summer season it is open every day except Monday, in the winter by appointment; phone 889–9440. Admission is fifty cents, children free if accompanied by an adult.

BEDROOM, LEFFINGWELL INN

45

LYMAN HOUSE

WALTHAM, MASSACHUSETTS

The elegant country house built in Waltham for Theodore Lyman is a rare specimen. It is the only one of the country houses designed by the famous architect Samuel McIntire that stands today. Two later alterations by the Lyman family, one in 1884 and one in 1917, have their own architectural interest. Furthermore, the garden setting for The Vale represents one of the few landscaped estates surviving from the early nineteenth-century, well documented and almost unaltered. Within the grounds stand two greenhouses dating from 1800 and 1804—also somewhat unusual in America.

Original drawings in the Essex Institute reveal a scheme for a main unit with a kitchen wing, a scheme that was redesigned before construction into a well-balanced arrangement typical of contemporary English houses: main unit with two wings, each connected to the house by a hyphen. In 1882, after living in the mansion for almost a hundred years, the Lyman family engaged the services of a Boston architect, Henry W. Hartwell, to transform the country seat into an imposing mansion. A large kitchen wing and a third story were added to the main house, the hyphens were raised in height, and bay windows were projected. Indoors, the stairs were relocated and the original kitchen was made into a music room. With just two exceptions—the great ballroom and the bow parlor—the rooms in the house were overlaid with woodwork in the style of Mr. Hartwell's contemporary, H. H. Richardson. Left unaltered, those two rooms still reveal McIntire's original handiwork. The fondness for the old style prompted the family to retain the two rooms, which led to a restoration in 1917 for which Mr. Arthur Lyman turned to a Miss N. D. Tupper. She removed the Victorian overlay in the main rooms and substituted the forms of the full-blown Colonial Revival. Thus, in addition to the McIntire tradition in the bow parlor and ballroom, we find the rich forms of the Richardson school in the music rooms and staircase, and in the dining room and east parlor there is the interesting restoration of 1917.

Although we know little of the particular formal program to set out the grounds, and almost nothing of Mr. William Bell, the English gardener hired by Theodore Lyman, the landscaping of The Vale illustrates the informal naturalistic style popularized by Sir Humphrey Repton. This style was intended to improve on the natural setting by such devices as extending lawns, opening vistas through woods, enlarging streams into picturesque ponds, building a ha-ha. The Vale's fine trees, ponds, one-time deer park, extensive lawns sweeping from the house to the ponds, and the pleasure garden behind the house extending to the foot of the hill show the application of Repton's principles to this fine country seat.

Marking the base of the hill is a wall and the old greenhouse, built about 1804. Behind it in the kitchen garden stands its predecessor, which was built about 1800. The older greenhouse has survived largely intact with its original flue arrangement and wrought-iron firebox fittings. In the second greenhouse original masonry walls are intact, and traces of the original flues are visible. But, through the years modifications were made to keep up to date with greenhouse procedures, for the structure houses old camellias and a Black Hamburg grapevine imported from Hampton Court about 1870.

Threatened subdivision of the property and destruction of the mansion and its subordinate buildings, including the McIntire stable, led five descendants of the original builder, Theodore Lyman, to bequeath the mansion and thirty acres of land to the Society for the Preservation of New England Antiquities, which is refurbishing the property and has opened it to the public.

LYMAN HOUSE is located on Lyman Street in Waltham, Massachusetts. It can be reached by turning off Route 20 in the center of Waltham onto Lyman Street. The house is on the right on the other side of the railroad tracks. It is open from Thursday through Saturday from 11:00 A.M. to 5:00 P.M. from May 21 to August 29. The admission charge is fifty cents.

THE MOFFATT-LADD HOUSE

PORTSMOUTH, NEW HAMPSHIRE

Captain John Moffat, builder of the Moffatt-Ladd House, first came into Portsmouth harbor in 1723 as captain of one of the ships that loaded at Portsmouth with masts for the royal navy. Attracted by the activity and promise of the place, he resigned his command to become a resident, married Miss Sarah Cutt, daughter of one of the leading families, and prospered as a ship owner. His son, Samuel, graduated from Harvard in the class of 1758 and then engaged in business, which took him frequently to England. There he met and wooed the daughter of his father's old friend, John Mason. Captain John Moffatt was proud of the forthcoming wedding and decided to give the couple as handsome a house as money could build. Portsmouth had no professional architect, but she had highly skilled ship carpenters to do the job. The house was completed in 1763, and on February 1, 1764, Samuel Moffatt and his bride took possession.

It was a prosperous time to start life. Land speculation was lively, and trade with the increasing population brought new wealth to Portsmouth. Fashions and furnishings came from England, and Copley portraits show the grace and elegance with which the handsome citizens of Portsmouth wore their imported finery. The young Moffatts belonged to this inner circle, and for a few years their mansion played its part with gay hospitality. According to one contemporary chronicler, Samuel Moffatt's "college education and fashionable life had not qualified him for strict and prudent application to business," and he became heavily indebted and was in danger from that strange judicial system that made recovery impossible by locking up the debtor. Samuel escaped imprisonment by flight. He parted from his wife, his two little sons, and his beautiful house. He slipped away on the brig *Diana,* whose captain, William Whipple, was suitor to Samuel's sister, Miss Catherine Moffatt. Samuel made a fresh start in the West Indies, and there his family followed him, never again to live in the mansion built for them.

DINING ROOM, MOFFATT-LADD HOUSE

John Moffatt, then a widower, had in settlement of his son's affairs bought back the mansion, and he took residence there with his daughter, Catherine. Captain William Whipple's wooing of Catherine Moffatt prospered, and after they were married, they lived with Captain Moffatt. William Whipple left the sea to establish himself as a merchant and to take part in provincial affairs in the troubled time preceding the Revolution. He was active in the Revolution, and in 1776 he was sent to the Continental Congress at Philadelphia; he was one of the signers of the Declaration of Independence. In 1777 he led New Hampshire troops at the battle of Saratoga. At the end of the war he ranked as a major general.

The Whipples, who were childless, continued to live with the aged Captain Moffatt. The house became one of the centers of the social and political life of the new state. General Whipple was appointed a judge of the Superior Court of New Hampshire. Also living at the mansion was Mary Tufton Moffatt, daughter of the refugee Samuel. At the age of seventeen she eloped with Dr. Haven, a rising physician of the town. When General Whipple died at the age of fifty-six, Dr. and Mrs. Haven bought the house for their daughter on her marriage to Alexander Ladd. The son of this marriage, Alexander Hamilton Ladd, was the last of the family to pass his entire life in the Moffatt-Ladd House. In 1913 the house was leased to the Society of Colonial Dames in New Hampshire, who assumed responsibility for its conservation.

The Moffatt-Ladd House is wood framed clapboard with quoined corners. The roof is topped by a deck, the popular Captain's or Widow's Walk surrounded by a handsome balustrade with urn pinials. On the first floor the windows are surmounted by segmental pediments. Those on the second floor have elaborate swan-necked pediments, each terminating in a pair of conventionalized Tudor roses. The third-floor windows meet the cornice. This was the first three-story houses in Portsmouth. A flight of ten granite steps leads up to the porch. When Captain Moffatt planned the house, he sacrificed a front room for "a great hall in the English sense." This Hall is certainly the finest in New England. To the right there is a flight of stairs, the box-paneled ends supported by richly carved brackets and each carrying in succession a turned, a twisted, and a fluted baluster topped by a rail. The walls are covered with a rare wallpaper known as The Bay of Naples paper, printed by Joseph Dufour in Paris between 1815 and 1820.

In the drawing room, which opens at the back of the Hall, the mantel panel is adorned with a delicately carved festoon of flowers in high relief. The three windows, all in the back wall, look out on the upward slope of the garden. The curtains are supposed to be the originals. They were found stored in a chest upstairs. The dining room opens from the hall at the left of the front door and looks on the street. An arched recess accommodates the sideboard. The mantel is elaborate, and the opening of the fireplace is surrounded by English tiles. The pantry, opening from the right side of the room, contains a flight of stairs leading to the wine cellar and enclosed with a folding partition that transforms into a counter when not in use. The kitchen has an array of paneled cupboards and a huge woodshed in the long ell. The landing of the front staircase is adorned by a paneled window seat with imposing round-arched window flanked by rich pilasters. The staircase ends in an upper hall with coved ceiling. From this opens the long and narrow Ship Room. The spacious master bedroom has no north windows and looks out on the garden. Originally there was a wallpaper with a pattern of hunting scenes. Four of these sheets survive. Two smaller rooms with passage and back stairs complete this floor. These rooms have elaborate overmantel panels and pleasant window seats with folding shutters. The one overlooking the garden is the "President's Room." The rooms on the third floor are unused.

The present furniture of the mansion consists of purchases by the Society of Colonial Dames and gifts or loans by the members. In the hall are two Flemish scroll chairs with cane backs. The walnut lowboy dates from about 1680. Two Queen Anne chairs and one of the mid-century lead to a sofa of the Hepplewhite type in the hall. Near the angle of the stairs stands a large gate-legged table. Other choice pieces in the mansion are Windsor chairs, a rare stretcher table, and a high stool.

The grounds include a formal garden dating from the time the house was built, a coach house, and a counting house added in 1800.

The MOFFATT-LADD HOUSE is located on 154 Market Street in Portsmouth, New Hampshire, overlooking the Piscataqua River. It is open from May 15 to October 15. The admission is fifty cents for adults and twenty-five cents for children.

UPPER HALL, MOFFATT-LADD HOUSE

51

MYSTIC, CONNECTICUT

Mystic Seaport is not a restoration but a re-creation of a typical early New England coastal village of the mid-nineteenth century. This re-created maritime community was built on thirty acres bordering the historic Mystic River—historic because of ship-building industries that flourished on its banks a century ago.

Mystic Seaport was planned as a living, active, seafaring community designed to show the visitor the actual conditions under which American seamen once lived and worked. Its cobbled waterfront street is lined with authentic and original buildings and lofts and shops typical of those from which square-rigged whalers and clipper ships once were fitted out for long voyages at sea.

Crafts and skills prevailing in the period Mystic Seaport represents, including blacksmithing, sailmaking, netmaking, printing, woodcarving, are manifest throughout the grounds; actual demonstrations of skills are given, and products are sold to visitors.

A walk down curving Village Street, a rough dirt road with a flagstone walk, leads the visitor past the green, the Fishtown Chapel, and the Boardman Schoolhouse. This setting of charm and simplicity gives a vivid impression of our spiritual and cultural heritage from the mid-nineteenth century.

A ride in a horse-drawn "barge" along a waterfront street will take the visitor past the century-old whaleship that is berthed along Seaport Street, the *Charles W. Morgan,* last surviving whaling ship. There one can see the *Joseph Conrad,* a famous training ship built in Copenhagen in 1882, the Danish ketch *Gundel,* the exploration schooner *Bowdoin,* retired after twenty-six voyages to the Arctic, and the Gloucester fisherman *L.A. Dunton;* all have reached their port of call. There are numerous small craft, some the only existing examples of their types, on exhibit throughout the grounds.

The Seaport Museum houses many maritime treasures that document the lives of ships and men whose contributions to American history

RIGGED YOUTH TRAINING SHIP JOSEPH CONRAD, MYSTIC SEAPORT

VIEW OF CURVING SEAPORT STREET, MYSTIC SEAPORT

FISHTOWN CHAPEL AND BOARDMAN SCHOOLHOUSE, MYSTIC SEAPORT

have been great. The Library is specialized for research in maritime history; it has a catalogue of notable imprints and a large manuscript collection related to ships and the sea and allied industries. The Seaport Planetarium offers daily lecture-demonstrations. Through the most modern equipment, the ancient science of celestial navigation is defined.

Mystic Seaport is located on Route 27 in Mystic, Connecticut. It is open daily from 9:00 A.M. to 5:00 P.M. except Thanksgiving and Christmas days. Admission charges are listed by Mystic Seaport as "moderate." There are no specific prices given.

VIEW OF NORTH PARADE WHARF AND CRUISING CLUB, MYSTIC SEAPORT

NICKELS-SORTWELL HOUSE

WISCASSET, MAINE

The imposing and gracefully beautiful Nickels-Sortwell House represents a transitory moment of success and grandeur in the life of the town of Wiscasset. At the beginning of the nineteenth century Wiscasset hit the high point of its history. After incorporation in 1760 there developed an export trade, particularly in lumber. At the turn of the nineteenth century Wiscasset had begun to reap the harvest of American neutrality during the Napoleonic wars, when ships flying the American flag could enter European ports. Shipbuilding and trading brought constant activity to Wiscasset's sheltered inland port. But with Napoleon's decrees of Berlin and Milan and Great Britain's retaliating Order in Council in 1807, American commerce was cut off from the high seas; ship owners and their employees in Wiscasset were among the many who suffered severe losses as a result.

The Nickels-Sortwell House was built for Captain William Nickels, a returned mariner whose re-entry into commerce and navigation led to the prosperity that enabled him to erect his mansion on Main Street. He had owned the original house on the site; but with prosperity he had had the old one rolled back and in 1807–08 had a new one built. The cost of his new mansion was $14,000—a small fortune at that time. Tradition says that it took one man two years to finish the front hall and that it required the services of another to keep the hearths supplied with wood in the winter.

In proportions and details the Nickels-Sortwell House shows the influence of the style of Charles Bulfinch and a refined decorativeness. The center of the façade is characterised by a tripartite scheme such as that in the first Harrison Gray Otis House in Boston; it is a design of gradated forms—door with fanlight, sidelights and porch, Palladian window on the sec-

ond floor, and curved fanlight on the third. Delicate metal tracery adorns the glass. Thin Corinthian columns supporting the porch repeat the Corinthian pilasters that course up the walls between the windows. Arches above the two inner windows on the first floor echo those of the central scheme and remind us of the colonnade that spreads across the façade of the State House in Boston. The herringbone carving of the doorway pilasters and the gradation of reeds and darts in the arch from the center represent two unusual features of the house's design. Within, we find an elliptical hallway and handsome circular staircase, features heightened by the quality of their restrained ornamental carving.

Soon after the completion of the Nickels House in 1812, Captain Nickels' only daughter died at the age of ten years, and within the year her mother died. The bereaved captain survived only a few years, and his heirs sold his mansion. Its purchaser, Cornelius Turner, was but the first of a line of owners who employed the house as a hostelry and tavern until 1900; during that period it was known as Turner's Tavern, Belle Haven, and Wiscasset House. In 1900 Alvin Sortwell bought it, restored it to its original function—that of a home—and filled it with family furniture and furnishings. The Sortwell family willed it to the Society for the Preservation of New England Antiquities, which has opened it to the public, complete with all the family's collection.

The NICKELS-SORTWELL HOUSE is located on Main and Federal Streets in Wiscasset, Maine. It can be reached by Route 1, about 52 miles north of Portland. It is open from Tuesday through Saturday from 11:00 A.M. to 5:00 P.M. and on Sunday from 2:00 P.M. to 5:00 P.M. It is open from mid-June to mid-October. The admission charge is fifty cents.

OLD DEERFIELD

DEERFIELD, MASSACHUSETTS

Once white man's farthest outpost in the wilderness, Old Deerfield is remarkable today for its tranquil beauty, its courageous, blood-stained place in American history, and its famous mile-long village street lined with historic houses that give us a close glimpse of the life, manners, and surroundings of the eighteenth-century citizens. These houses are fortunately undesecrated by the invasion of later architectural styles.

The extraordinary village of Old Deerfield is a living monument to early America. It is a tribute to Deerfield's hard-bitten farmers, who were eager collectors of china, glassware, silver, pewter, and fabrics. They lived in a period of discriminating good taste. They commissioned capable artists to paint their family portraits. They were willing buyers of fine furniture, particularly that produced in their own Connecticut Valley. The houses and their furnishings are excellent examples of Colonial good taste in furniture, interior decoration, and architecture.

Among the buildings lining the mile-long village street is the Reverend Jonathan Ashley House. From 1732 to 1780 this gambreled-roofed house was the residence of the Rev. Jonathan Ashley, widely known on the frontier as an aggressive preacher, an incorrigible Loyalist, and a militant Tory. Removed from its foundation to be used as a tobacco barn, the house has been returned to its original site and restored to its original design. It is furnished with outstanding seventeenth- and eighteenth-century furniture and accessories, including eighteenth-century Deerfield crewelwork and a block-front secretary.

The Sheldon Hawks House was built in 1743 as the residence of the late George Sheldon, historian of Deerfield. It was owned by the Sheldon family for two centuries. Its structural features include all the original fine paneling and a dual-approach rear stairway. Among the furnishings are numerous family pieces. The china includes Delft, Worcester, Leeds, and Whieldon and pewter, figurines, toys, and baskets.

The Wright House, one of the only two brick houses in Deerfield, was built by Asa Stebbins and erected for his son, Asa Jr., in 1824. The name of the house is taken from that of its second owner. In it are some of the noted Cluett collection of furniture, mostly of the Federal

ASA STEBBINS HOUSE, OLD DEERFIELD

SHELDON HAWKS HOUSE, OLD DEERFIELD

period, including pieces by John Seymour, Samuel McIntire, Duncan Phyfe, and Thomas Sheraton.

The Parker & Russell Silver Shop was built by the Clesson family in 1814. Isaac Parker was a Deerfield silversmith during the Revolution, and John Russell, of an old Deerfield family, was his apprentice. The craft of the silversmith is demonstrated, and there is an exhibition of early American silver.

When it was completed in the 1790s for the son of the richest landowner in the county, the Asa Stebbins House was considered the showplace of the village. The house is a fine setting for the delicate late eighteenth- and early-nineteenth-century Hepplewhite and Sheraton furniture. Included in the furnishings are pieces attributed to John Seymour and Samuel McIntire and portraits by Gilbert Stuart, John Greenwood, and others. Throughout the house are contemporary and earlier ceramics, glassware, rugs, and other accessories. There are hand-painted wall decorations in the dining room and pantry, and on the walls of the bedrooms are examples of swag-type wallpaper.

The Frary House dates from the late seventeenth century. During the Revolutionary War it was a center of Whig activity. The first meeting of the trustees of Deerfield Academy was held there in 1797. It is used as an Inn today. Wellsthorn, its central section, was constructed about 1717 and has been restored as the simple home of an early eighteenth-century pioneer, Ebenezer Wells. By 1751 the Indian threat had passed, and Wells, a well-to-do farmer, merchant, and tavernkeeper, added the front section in the taste of the mid-century

The south rooms retain the original paneling and are furnished with Deerfield items. In 1801 Hezekiah Wright Strong installed his lawyer's office upstairs.

The Dwight Barnard House, built by Josiah Dwight in 1754, was rescued from wreckers in Springfield, Massachusetts, and rebuilt on its present site. Its architectural kinship with many of the houses along the village street is easily recognized. The superbly proportioned rooms, the large living-room-type kitchen, and unusual fireplace with cooking facilities are noteworthy, as is the unusual grained paneling in the south bedroom. One room is set up as a doctor's office with the possessions of Thomas Williams and his son, William Stoddard Williams, who collectively served the community for approximately one hundred years.

Other points of interest in Old Deerfield are Memorial Hall, the Wilson Printing House, the Broom Shop, Liberty Pole, the Memorial Stones, Old Fort Well, the old churches, the three Old Deerfield Private Schools, and the Civil War Monument.

OLD DEERFIELD is located in Deerfield, Massachusetts. It is open from May 1 to November 1, and some buildings are open the entire year. It is open daily from 9:30 A.M. to 12:00 noon and from 1:30 P.M. to 4:30 P.M. and on Sundays from 1:30 P.M. to 4:40 P.M. Admission to each building is $1.00 except the Wilson Printing House—twenty-five cents. Frary House—seventy-five cents, Memorial Hall—seventy-five cents and Indian House Memorial—fifty cents.

DWIGHT BARNARD HOUSE, OLD DEERFIELD

Old Sturbridge Village is a regional center of living history. Its purposes are historical and educational—the preservation and presentation of the story of New England farm and village life of yesterday and the dissemination of knowledge and understanding of that heritage to the citizens of today.

The Village is not a restoration of an actual historical place but the recreation of a representative New England community of the period 1790 to 1840. The Village was laid out on a two-hundred-acre tract of farmland through which flows the Quinebaug River to form the ponds, for the saw and grist mill. It was laid out in a typical village plan with its common, roads and paths, and to it were brought the more than thirty-five major buildings.

An organized stroll around Old Sturbridge Village will bring the visitor to the Friends (Quaker) Meeting House, which was built in 1796 for the Society of Friends in Bolton, Massa-

STEPHEN FITCH HOUSE, OLD STURBRIDGE

OLD STURBRIDGE VILLAGE

WRIGHT'S GRIST MILL, OLD STURBRIDGE

chusetts. Its unadorned simplicity reflects the spirit of the New England Quakers. The Village Meeting House is a local example of early Greek revival architecture. It was built in Sturbridge in 1832. The Militia Powder House was built in 1806 at Oxford, Massachusetts, for the storage of militia powder and shot. The Hitchcock Boot Shop contains bootmaker's and cobbler's tools, benches and lasts, and examples of early handcrafted footwear. The Schoolhouse came from Candia, New Hampshire, where it was in service until 1885. The Pottery Shop was

PARLOR, GENERAL SALEM TOWNE HOUSE, OLD STURBRIDGE

built about 1814 at Goshen, Connecticut, and operated until the late 1860s. Freeman Farm recreates life on a small New England farm. The Tin and Broom Shop have actual demonstrations of these crafts. Moses Wilder Blacksmith Shop, an unusual granite structure, was built about 1820 at Bolton, Massachusetts. Iron is wrought there at a two-man forge. Wight's Grist Mill is reproduced on the site of the original Wight Mill. Buckwheat, wheat, rye, corn, and graham flours are stone ground and bagged. The Cheney Up-and-Down Saw Mill is the type

GENERAL SALEM TOWNE HOUSE, OLD STURBRIDGE

FIREPLACE IN KITCHEN OF JOHN FENNO HOUSE, OLD STURBRIDGE

that cut trees into boards for eighteenth-century building and furniture making. It is from Gilead, Connecticut. The Covered Bridge was built at Dummerston, Vermont, where it spanned the Taft River for many decades. The Village Tavern was the hospitable part of the village. This tavern also houses collections of lighting devices, woodenware, early New England art, and a barroom.

One of the major buildings is the Richardson House, built in Podunk, East Brookfield, Massachusetts, about 1748. It is an excellent example of a "salt-box" house of eighteenth-century New England. The Lawyer's Office is a one-room

DINING ROOM, SALT BOX HOUSE, OLD STURBRIDGE

structure built in 1810 at Woodstock, Connecticut, by Judge John McClellan and used until his death in 1858. The John Fenno House was erected in 1704 at Canton, Massachusetts. It is the oldest house in the Village. The Stephen Fitch House dates from 1737. It was moved from Willimantic, Connecticut. Candle dipping and candle molding are demonstrated in the summer kitchen. The Thompson Bank is a brick and granite Greek revival building that was a banking building in Thompson, Connecticut, from 1835 until the early 1890s. Miner Grant's General Store lasted well into the latter part of the nineteenth century in Stafford, Con-

necticut. It displays many old-time wares. Gen. Salem Towne House was built in 1796 by General Salem Towne in Charlton, Massachusetts. It reflects the finest country craftsmanship of which New England was capable. The Isaiah Thomas Printing Office was built at Worcester. Massachusetts, in the 1780s by the famous New England printer and publisher of the Massachusetts *Spy*.

Other buildings include the Glass Exhibit, the Bake House, the Pewter Shop, Guns and Wrought Iron in New England, the Clock Exhibit, and the Cabinet Shop.

JOHN FENNO HOUSE, OLD STURBRIDGE

PARLOR, SALT BOX HOUSE, OLD STURBRIDGE

OLD STURBRIDGE VILLAGE is at the junction of Routes 15 and 20 and the Massachusetts Turnpike in Sturbridge, Massachusetts. From April through November all buildings are open from 9:30 A.M. to 5:30 P.M. every day. From December through March there are guided tours on weekdays at 10:00 A.M. and 2:00 P.M. The Village is fully open on Saturdays and Sundays. Admission for adults is $2.50, children 8–17, $1.00, children under 8 free.

STEPHEN FITCH HOUSE, OLD STURBRIDGE

HARRISON GRAY OTIS HOUSE

BOSTON, MASSACHUSETTS

In 1916, when the Society for the Preservation of New England Antiquities acquired this house for its headquarters, only a trained eye could have recognized its architectural and historical impressiveness. Its fine façade lay hidden behind a row of little shops; the line of the roof was broken by two peaked dormers; the Palladian window, fanlight, semicircular porch with Corinthian columns, the old twelve-pane windows (six-pane on the third floor)—all now authentically restored—had been ripped off and replaced with clumsy features as inappropriate to the structure as was the conversion into a rooming house of this splendid late eighteenth-century town dwelling of Boston's third mayor, Harrison Gray Otis, lawyer, businessman, and statesman.

Careful research went into the restoration and furnishing of this building, so that visitors now view an authentic period piece, the only brick house of that day that still stands in Boston. Together with its next-door neighbor, the Old West Church designed by Asher Benjamin, the Otis House represents the remnants of Boston's otherwise demolished West End. Its front windows look across Cambridge Street to the panoply of Beacon Hill, and toward the west a fragment of the span of the Charles River remains visible.

The structure has been attributed to Charles Bulfinch not only because of the close association of Otis and the architect but also because of stylistic congruence. Its appearance has simplicity and grandeur, for the mass of brick is broken only by symmetrically placed windows, belt courses between stories, quoins above the rectangular windows, and the series of doorway, Palladian window, and fanlight that ornaments the center of the façade.

The interior of the house itself is remarkably pleasant for two reasons. First, the high ceilings and large windows gives rooms of airy spaciousness and light. Second, the furnishings and decoration present an accurate image of the sub-tle and dignified style of the period. Carved plaster moldings and carved dados edge the walls, and mantels with applied plaster designs in the style of the English Adam brothers ornament the fireplaces.

In the dining room, for example, removal of layers of paint revealed the original scheme of cream-colored swags, rosettes, and mythological figures against a green ground. In the parlor white walls are trimmed with light green dados and woodwork. The upholstery on the Sheraton sofa and the Hepplewhite chairs as well as the window hangings are of the same fabric, a handsome red and gold damask that reproduces an eighteenth-century design and which was woven in France specially for the fiftieth anniversary of the Society.

The music room on the second floor boasts a pale yellow wallpaper with colorful floral borders along the moldings and chocolate-brown woodwork; this scheme, together with the appropriate old harp and piano, shows us the room almost exactly as it was when the Otises entertained friends there. Other interesting wallpapers—the "Captain Cook" wallpaper and the "Paysage Indien" paper, printed after 1804 by Dufour of Paris and Macon, France—hang in the chamber above the parlor. In others of the eight restored rooms there are equally authentic color schemes, window and bed hangings, furniture, paintings, china, and other accessories. The Society provides yet further insights into old-time New England through its exhibit of architectural elements and its museum of china, pottery, glass, pewter, costumes, and toys in the buildings annexed to the rear of the Harrison Gray Otis House.

The HARRISON GRAY OTIS HOUSE is located at 141 Cambridge Street in Boston, Massachusetts. It is entered from Lynde Street. It is open weekdays the year round from 10:00 A.M. to 4:00 P.M. Closed Saturdays, Sundays and holidays. The admission charge is fifty cents.

ROCKY HILL MEETINGHOUSE

AMESBURY, MASSACHUSETTS

In 1716 the west parish of the Massachusetts town of Salisbury—now Amesbury—separated from the older part of town. A meetinghouse was built, but by 1780 it had fallen into serious disrepair. Rather than renovating it, the church fathers decided to build a new meetinghouse, and the committee appointed by the town meeting set out to consider a new location. After several lively town meetings and bitter opposition from parishioners to the north, the site was selected and the Rocky Hill Meetinghouse that we see today was erected in 1785.

It looks much as it did when it was built. Although one might wonder whether this results from careful rebuilding on the part of the present owner, the Society for the Preservation of New England Antiquities, the meetinghouse came into the Society's hands with remarkably few alterations on the part of intervening generations; for shortly after its construction the congregation began to diminish. Those annoyed by the change of site found other meetinghouses to attend; the Great Awakening made further inroads, as members went to other fellowships. Nevertheless, the society was able to support a minister, though not to alter the structure, until the end of the nineteenth century. The meetinghouse witnessed the marriage of the parishioner Abigail Eastman to Ebenizer Webster, a widower from Salisbury, New Hampshire; one of their three children was Daniel Webster.

The meetinghouse survives as a rare example of the simplicity of early houses of worship. It is thought to have been built by Timothy Palmer of Newburyport, the designer of the meetinghouse of the First Religious Society in that town. From the outside the Rocky Hill structure resembles nothing so much as a house, albeit one with three doors, for it has no belfry or steeple. Dentilated cornices and very modestly carved doorways are the sole ornaments to its exterior.

Except for carving on the pulpit and its pentagonal sounding board, the plain interior demonstrates the feeling of the period that a meetinghouse should be a place where a man can concentrate on nothing but the sermon and the state of his soul. The room is flooded with light. The desire for the plain and natural is further demonstrated in the uncovered timbers of the roof frames and the woodwork; only the pillars supporting the gallery, the pulpit, and the face of the gallery are painted. Box pews of handsome aged pine cover the floor, and a gallery where the young men and women sat facing each other overhangs the room on three sides.

After many years of disuse, memorial services are now held in the Meetinghouse on three Sundays in the summer. The Society for the Preservation of New England Antiquities has recently acquired the parsonage and has moved it across the road to the Meetinghouse property, out of the path of the new highway. The parsonage was standing years before the Meetinghouse was erected and is a good example of a typical modest eighteenth-century house. It housed all the Meetinghouse's ministers, including Dr. Samuel Webster.

ROCKY HILL MEETINGHOUSE is located in Amesbury, Massachusetts. It can be reached from Newburyport Route 113 into State Route 95. From Boston Toll Road 95 between Amesbury and Salisbury north of Route 110. It is open weekdays from 9:00 A.M. to 5:00 P.M. from May through October. There is no admission charge, only a voluntary contribution.

DRAWING ROOM, RUGGLES HOUSE

COLUMBIA FALLS, MAINE

Standing practically the same as when it was built a century and a third ago, the Ruggles House is reminiscent of "an exotic elegance, and in its wistful charm, it is like the ghost of a dainty old lady, dressed in gray silk, who, having wandered out of the past, had sat down by the roadside and forgotten to go back."

The Ruggles House, constructed after a design by Aaron Sherman of Duxbury, Massachusetts, was built for Judge Thomas Ruggles, a wealthy lumber dealer, store owner, postmaster, prominent citizen, captain of militia, and justice of the Court of Sessions.

Ruggles House has been admired by architects and craftsmen. Among its many notable architectural features is the flying staircase rising from the center of the wide hall without lateral support to the landing and then dividing into two half flights, one to the right and one to the left. The woodcarving in the house was done by an English woodcarver who worked with a penknife for three years. Much of the work is extraordinarily delicate.

RUGGLES HOUSE is a quarter mile off U.S. Route 1 at Columbia Falls, Maine, and 41 miles east of Ellsworth, Maine. It is open from June 1 to September 30 on weekdays from 8:30 A.M. to 4:30 P.M. and Sundays from 12:30 A.M. to 4:00 P.M. Admission is fifty cents, children twenty-five cents.

MASTER BEDROOM, RUGGLESHOUSE

RUGGLES HOUSE

COLONEL JOSIAH QUINCY HOUSE

WOLLASTON, MASSACHUSETTS

Colonel Josiah Quincy was a prominent merchant and patriot in town and colonial affairs. He worked with Thomas Pownall to check southward movements of the French from Canada. His son Josiah Jr., was a noted patriot and orator; he died at sea in 1775 while returning from England, where he had gone to plead the cause of the colonies. His niece Dorothy married John Hancock. After his death his widow and son, Josiah III, spent only their summers at the house. Josiah III spent sixteen summers of his presidency of Harvard College at the house and entertained many of the great men of the time. He willed the house to his unmarried daughters. In 1896 the house and some of the land passed to Mrs. Edward R. Hall. She donated the deed to the Society for the Preservation of New England Antiquities.

The house is an impressive example of architecture. The hallway, nine feet wide, extends from the front door to the carriage door at the rear. It has paneled wainscoting and handsome cornices. The west parlor has fine paneled wainscoting on three sides, the fourth side being entirely paneled around the fireplace.

On the second floor the southwest chamber has a paneled wainscot and fine cornice. The north wall is paneled about the fireplace, which has a General Wolfe memorial fireback and painting. The tiles of terra cotta red are on a gray-blue ground. Other chambers have paneled wainscotting and moulded cornices.

The COLONEL JOSIAH QUINCY HOUSE is located at 20 Muirhead Street in Wollaston, Massachusetts. It can be reached from Boston by Route C37 to Route 6. It is open on Tuesday, Thursday, and Friday from 1:00 P.M. to 5:00 P.M. from May to mid-October. The admission charge is twenty-five cents.

CUSTOM HOUSE, SALEM MARITIME

SALEM, MASSACHUSETTS

Founded in 1626 by Roger Conant as the plantation of Naumkeag and established two years later as the first town in the Colony of Massachusetts Bay, Salem owed its early start to its seaboard location. From the start her colonists engaged in maritime pursuits and soon made fishing and shipping the leading industries of the community. As early as 1643 fish, lumber, and provisions were being sent to the West Indies in exchange for sugar and molasses, staples that were brought home and made into rum. Gradually the orbit of trade was extended to Europe, for the most part to Portugal and Spain, which offered ready markets for dried fish and supplied salt, wine, fruit, iron, and Spanish dollars in return.

This trade thrived until 1763, when the government of England began to enforce new measures to limit the commercial intercourse of the American Colonies. Under these conditions the economic life of Salem, like that of other continental ports along the Atlantic seaboard, was brought to a standstill. This fostered a discontent that grew into resistance and resulted in rebellion. During the Revolution, Salem gave aid to the colonial cause by privateering directed against British commerce. Salem was the one American continental port of significance that did not fall into the hands of the British at any time during the war. From 1776 to 1782 Salem averaged fifty vessels continually at sea preying on enemy shipping and engaging enemy ships.

At the end of the war Salem made a world-wide search for new markets, going as far as the East Indies and China; these voyages (lasting as long as two years) helped usher in the first golden age of American foreign trade and achieved for Salem the reputation of a "New World Venice." Again Salem was to get a fatal blow; the embargo President Jefferson imposed on American shipping in 1807 and the War of 1812 were the first of several factors that led to her decline. With the decade of the clipper ship in 1850–60, Salem's maritime career was brought to a close. Her land-locked harbor was too shallow to accommodate the large new ships, and her commerce was absorbed by the deep-water ports of Boston and New York.

Derby Wharf, which extends nearly 2,000 feet into Salem Harbor, is one of the important survivals from the great days of Salem shipping. It was begun by Capt. Richard Derby soon after 1762, and during the Revolution was used by his son, Elias Hasket Derby, as a base for fitting out privateers. After the war the wharf became one of the great mercantile centers of the young republic. Trade with Europe, the East Indies, and China centered around Derby Wharf. After 1800 the wharf suffered a century of neglect until it was reconstructed by the National Park Service in 1938.

Directly opposite Derby Wharf is the Customs House, built in 1819. Nathaniel Hawthorne worked there as Surveyor of the Port of Salem from 1846 to 1849. The desk and other objects used by Hawthorne have been preserved. In the southeast room of the Customs House are exhibits and panels illustrating the history of Salem's ocean-going commerce.

The Derby House, now the oldest brick dwelling in Salem, was erected in 1761–62 by Capt. Richard Derby for his son, Elias Hasket Derby. The latter was married in 1761 and occupied the house until the early years of the Revolutionary War. A later resident was Capt. Henry Prince, a master in the Derby fleet. Some interior restoration has been necessary. The original paint colors of the various rooms and the ornate staircase in the front hall are of unusual interest. Among the furnishings are objects associated with the Derbys.

The Rum Shop, a building probably erected in 1800 or soon after, stands on the corner east of the Derby House. The Hawkes House, just west of the Derby House was designed about 1780 by Samuel McIntire, Salem's great archi-

tect, as a sumptuous mansion for Elias Hasket Derby. Captain Benjamin Hawkes, a ship-builder and merchant, bought the structure in 1801 and completed it in its present form.

Extending into the harbor parallel to and west of Derby Wharf but only one third as long, is Central Wharf, constructed in 1791–92 by Aimon Forrester, captain of a Derby privateer in the Revolution and subsequently a prominent merchant. John Bertram, the last of the great Salem merchants to engage in worldwide trade, and his partners were in business at Central Wharf from 1840 to 1859, occupying a brick warehouse built by the family before 1832. The walls of the warehouse were reduced and stabilized in 1948.

RUM SHOP, SALEM MARITIME

SALEM MARITIME NATIONAL HISTORIC SITE is on Derby Street, Salem, Massachusetts, about twenty miles northeast of Boston. From Boston and points south it can be reached by State Routes 1A and 107 and also by State Route 129. It is open daily from 10:00 A.M. to 5:00 P.M. The "nominal" fee is waived for children under twelve.

81

SILAS DEANE HOUSE

WETHERSFIELD, CONNECTICUT

Silas Deane was born in Groton, Connecticut, on December 24, 1737. He graduated from Yale in 1758 and was admitted to the bar in 1761. He moved to Wethersfield, opened an office there, and not long after married the wealthy Widow Webb. They had one son, Jesse, born in 1764. Mrs. Deane died in 1767, and some time later Deane married Elizabeth Saltonstall.

Deane seems to have become an important member of the Wethersfield community soon after he arrived in the town. He served on many committees. He helped plan the surprise attack on Fort Ticonderoga and contributed money to finance the expedition. He was a member of the General Assembly of the New England states and in 1774 was sent to Philadelphia as a delegate from Connecticut to the Continental Congress. In March of 1776 he was sent to France by Congress as a secret agent to induce the French Government to lend financial aid to Congress. His commission was signed by Benjamin Franklin, Benjamin Harrison, John Dickinson, John Jay, and Robert Morris. In December, 1776, he was joined by Benjamin Franklin and Arthur Lee; all three were named Commissioners Plenipotentiary from the United States to the court of France. He remained abroad until 1789 and died aboard ship in Deal harbor, England, as he was about to return to America.

Silas Deane House differs in many respects from most of its contemporaries in Connecticut. It is an expression of both the personality of its owner and the ideas and ingenuity of his unknown builder. When young Deane married Joseph Webb's widow, he set about building a mansion proper to his status. Obviously, suitability for entertainment was the primary factor of design.

Across the entire front of the house and turning a short distance on each side was a piazza, or porch, the only prerevolutionary example in Connecticut. It was removed some years ago but will be restored. Evidence conclusively proves this structure to have existed. There is also a rear porch, less rare in Connecticut, portions of which still remain.

The entrance hall and staircase, with its curved banister, are among the finest in New England. They occupy nearly half the front part of the house and have no equal in Connecticut for spaciousness and elegance. All the rooms are larger, ceilings higher, and appointments finer than the average house of the 1760s.

The parlor fireplace is of Portland brownstone, carved in high relief and originally lined with Dutch tile. The huge kitchen has an enormous fireplace with two ovens. A stone sink in this room is probably the original, as are the big open cupboards.

SILAS DEANE HOUSE is located on Main Street in Wethersfield, Connecticut. The ground floor has just been opened for the public. Inquiries as to days and times of entry can be made at Webb House, next door.

83

NEWBURY, MASSACHUSETTS

Beginning with the 1651 ell, the Tristram Coffin House was developed through the seventeenth and eighteenth centuries. Its furnishings represent the possessions of one family for more than eight generations.

The first Tristram Coffin was a cavalier, the only royalist in the district. He came to the colonies in 1642 at the age of thirty-three with his mother, his two sisters, and his wife and five children, one of whom was the Tristram Jr. who named this house. The house was standing at the time of his marriage in 1653 and might have been built by his wife's father.

The Tristram Coffin House reveals its Gothic origins in its outward shape—the steep pitch of the roof, the relation of height of wall to height of the ridge. The heavy beams, massive fireplace, and width of board and plank are from a period when lumber was cut from endless virgin forests.

When Nathaniel, youngest son of Tristram Coffin Jr., married in 1699 and brought his wife to his father's house, the first addition to the house was built for his family—the south end of the present house. The Gothic style was forsaken, and a transition toward the classic began. The northeasterly end of the present house was apparently built about 1725, on the occasion of the marriage of Nathaniel's son Joseph. In floor plan and wall treatment this addition shows the dawning formality of the eighteenty century.

A charming feature of the house is the buttery, one of the few preserved intact, complete with churns, stools, wooden bowls, and even a milkmaid's yoke.

The TRISTRAM COFFIN HOUSE is located at 16 High Road in Newbury, Massachusetts. It is open on Monday, Wednesday, and Friday from 2:00 P.M. to 5:00 P.M. from mid-June through mid-September. Admission is twenty-five cents.

TRISTRAM COFFIN HOUSE

Webb House is situated on the broad Main Street of Wethersfield, one of the oldest settlements in Connecticut. It gives a picture of the eighteenth century, its development in architecture in Connecticut, and, with its present furnishings, an idea of the manner of the gracious living of that era. In addition, its part in the history of this country has been said to equal that of Faneuil Hall, the cradle of liberty, and of Independence Hall; for it was at Webb House, at the Yorktown Conference, that General George Washington laid the plans that resulted in the successful termination of the Revolutionary War. General Washington, the

Count de Rochambeau, General Henry Knox (aged thirty-one), who later became our first Secretary of War, and Colonel Jeremiah Wadsworth were among those who crowded into the parlor at that historic meeting. Webb House is said to be the only house still standing in America where Rochambeau spent the night.

Joseph Webb built his house in 1752, when he was twenty-five years old; he lived in it with his wife, Mehitabel Nott, for nine years. After his death Mrs. Webb married Silas Deane, a great patriot who went to France to enlist the sympathies of the Marquis de Lafayette in the American cause. They vacated Webb House for her

WEBB HOUSE

son Joseph Webb Jr. and his bride and went to live in the house Deane built, which is still standing next to Webb House (see *Silas Deane House*).

The architecture of Webb House is interesting. The house was built on property acquired from Major Samuel Wolcott II, and consisted of "dwelling house, barn, shop and all other buildings standing thereon." The exterior is well proportioned. It is a two-chimney house and has a fine gambrel roof. It has a small ell built in 1678. Tradition says that the ell of the house, now the kitchen, is the original Wolcott House. A white picket fence, recently rebuilt in accordance with a 1752 type of fence, encloses the front yard. The house was shaded then, as now, by elm trees. The front porch was added later. Webb House is a typical example of the central hall plan of the period with parlors on each side of the entrance. It is open and spacious inside. The brick terrace and garden beyond can be glimpsed through the hall and the open door at the rear.

There is fine paneling of the fireplace walls on the first and second floors. The back parlor has been repainted the same bright blue found on its walls when they were scraped. The same red flocked wallpaper is in the north chamber, which Washington occupied. The kitchen, with its huge fireplace, utensils of by-gone days, and great wide floor boards is an excellent restoration.

The furnishings are mostly gifts from the Connecticut Society of Colonial Dames members. Some of the china, silver, and furniture donated might have been used by the Webb family. There is the carved oak Webb chest in the lower hall made by Peter Blinn, a Connecticut River cabinetmaker, the Webb silver tea service, probably made by Wishart of New York, and some pieces of English china, white with brown lines, that belonged to Samuel Blatchley Webb. The two grandfather clocks are specimens of Connecticut River cabinetmaker's art, and the Hepplewhite sideboard in the dining room is from Northford, Connecticut. The gentleman's library has a lovely gaming table with chessmen. The council room contains two cherry Chippendale chairs and a tray-top Chippendale tea table with sliding ends used for candles. The china in the dining room is Chinese Export porcelain, fine examples of Crown and Sprig Derby and Newhall manufacture. The most prized furnishing is the pole screen in the front parlor, whose needlepoint dates from the second half of the seventeenth century. Upstairs there is a double-front ox-bow cherry chest of drawers made by one of the Chapin cousins, the most famous of Connecticut River cabinetmakers.

Webb House has a collection of rare books and one of textiles that is fine and well authenticated. In this collection are crewel embroidered bed-curtains dated 1730, 1740, 1750–1760 made by Mrs. John Chester, mother of Abigail Webb. The coverlet to this set of bed hangings is in the Metropolitan Museum of Art. Of historic interest in this collection is the piece of crewel embroidery that was formerly a gown em-

DINING ROOM, WEBB HOUSE

broidered circa 1750 by Anne Gray, wife of Colonel James Cralk of Lebanon, a soldier at Bunker Hill. On the beds and in the chests are hand-woven sheets and pillow cases.

The garden has plants that might have grown in a garden during the period of the Revolutionary War. The barn is the original old barn of the Webb House property, completely restored and now used for meetings and luncheons.

WEBB HOUSE is located on Main Street in Wethersfield, Connecticut. It is open daily except Sunday from 10:00 A.M. to 4:00 P.M. Admission is seventy-five cents.

FARMERS' MUSEUM AND FENIMORE HOUSE

COOPERSTOWN, NEW YORK

This unique restoration consists of not one but three related museums, each supplementing the other two. There is Fenimore House, The Farmers' Museum, and The Village Crossroads, a complex of eighteen buildings reflecting the life of people who lived in rural New York between 1783 and the 1840s. This entire restoration is managed by the New York State Historical Society. The Society's headquarters is in Fenimore House.

One enters this adventure in living history by way of a large stone dairy barn that has been converted into an indoor museum. The exhibits are tools of the farmer, his wife, and the craftsmen on which they depended. Objects were chosen and arranged to convey a feeling for how and with what the postfrontier folk made do. The Village Crossroads, where a dozen buildings have been brought together from a one-hundred-mile area, show what life was like in rural communities from 1783 to 1840. These buildings, moved with infinite care, serve the same function they served originally. The visitor will find the Blacksmith Shop (1827), the Printing Office (1829), the Druggist's Shop (1832), the Doctor's Office (1829), and the Lawyer's Office (actually the office of Samuel Nelson, later U. S. Supreme Court Justice). Across from these is Bump Tavern (c. 1800), a typical turnpike tavern, built in Ashland by Jehiel Tuttle. The roof of the tavern was raised and porches were added by Ephraim Bump in 1844. A little beyond these buildings, set in its own yard and attended by its pond and outbuildings, is the Lippitt Homestead (1797), a pioneer home built in nearby Hinman Hollow by Joseph Lippitt.

What is unique about this entire project is that wherever possible, the objects in all these recreations are shown in actual use. At Lippitt Farm, where flax and broom corn are grown, there are chickens, ducks, pigs, a few sheep, a team of oxen, and the family cow—just what the average farmer would have owned. There is a blacksmith in the smithy, the country store is in business and there is a printer in the Printing Office. There are demonstrations of woodworking, broommaking, spinning, and weaving.

Fenimore House, the Historical Society's headquarters, was built in 1932 on the site of a cottage once owned and occupied by James Fenimore Cooper. It contains a splendid collection of folk art—primitive paintings by John Brewster Jr., William Mathew Prior, Edward Hicks, Joseph Davis, Ruth Henshaw Bascom, Joseph Whiting Stock, and Erastus Salisbury Field. The roots of this collection are deeper in the craft tradition—woodcarving, metalwork, needlework, and scrimshaw. This is the kind of art known and enjoyed by the men and women who lived in similar communities.

FARMERS' MUSEUM AND FENIMORE HOUSE are in Cooperstown, New York, on New York Routes 80 and 28, thirty miles south of Exit 30 (from west) and Exit 29 (from east) on the New York Thruway. Fenimore House is open daily April 26 to June 30 from 9:00 A.M. to 6:00 P.M. During July and August it is open from 9:00 A.M. to 9:00 P.M.; from September 1 to November 1, from 9:00 A.M. to 6:00 P.M. Admission is seventy-five cents, children twenty-five cents.

Farmers' Museum is open daily April 26 to November 1 from 9:00 A.M. to 6:00 P.M. From November 2 to April 24 is is open from 9:00 A.M. to 5:00 P.M. The admission for Farmers' Museum is $1.25 for adults, twenty-five cents for children.

A combination ticket can be purchased for both for $1.75 for adults and forty cents for children. Both are closed Sunday mornings and all day Monday.

TROY, NEW YORK

The Hart-Cluett family mansion was designed by Philip Hooker and completed in 1827. It was built by William Howard of New York as a wedding present for his daughter Betsey Amelia Howard, who became the wife of Richard P. Hart. The Harts lived there until 1892, when the mansion became the property of George B. Cluett. In 1910 it became the property of the Albert E. Cluett, who lived here until 1952, when is was turned over to the Rensselaer County Historical Society for its permanent headquarters.

The original house is shown today in period rooms as it would have appeared in the 1830s and 1840s. The arched doorway and lintels of this delightful sandstone Federal house are trimmed with contrasting marble, which along the balustrade edging the eaves and round-headed dormers creates a sprightly appearance. The interior is even more charming; it has French scenic wallpaper in the entrance hall.

One of the fanciful features of the house is the repetition of the overdoor fanlight at every possible opportunity. Throughout the house all doorways and windows are flanked with acanthus leaf motif decorations.

There are priceless heirlooms in the mansion. The dining room is set with Sèvres china. The rare sideboard in the Empire style is by Elijah Galusha, Troy cabinetmaker. It is carved with pineapples, symbol of good hospitality. The convex mirror with Eagle decoration has been in the house since 1827. The Betsey Howard Hart Memorial Room is furnished in Duncan Phyfe style with pieces by Elijah Galusha. Carving on the graceful Galusha chaise lounge is in a wild rose pattern. The General Bradford Carr Memorial Room has a bedstead that belonged to Aaron Burr when he was Vice President of the United States. The champagne-colored satin hangings with crewel embroidery are original.

DINING ROOM

FRONT PARLOR

The HART-CLUETT family mansion is located at 59 Second Street in Troy, New York. It is open from Monday through Friday, 10:00 A.M. to 12 noon and from 2:00 P.M. to 5:00 P.M. Admission is free.

BETSY HOWARD HART MEMORIAL ROOM, HART-CLUETT FAMILY MANSION

HOPEWELL VILLAGE

RESTORED BARN, HOPEWELL

PENNSYLVANIA

Hopewell Village is one of the oldest ironworks standing in the country today. It is a symbol of industrial enterprise in early America and representative of the many furnaces of southeastern Pennsylvania. In the buildings of the village and in the restored furnace is one of the· best preserved examples of the forerunners of today's great iron and steel industry.

While the colonies struggled to establish themselves, capital was short and skills scarce. To avoid increasing their indebtedness to Europe, the colonists determined to make their own iron. Thus for nearly a hundred years most iron was made at bloomeries, which required little capital and few skilled workers.

As the colonies matured, large-scale industry became practical. Southeastern Pennsylvania, rich in iron ore, hardwood forests, limestone, and water power, became the leading iron-producing area. Charcoal smelting in this area began in Colebrookdale in 1720. When Mark Bird built Hopewell in 1770, there were at least nineteen other furnaces in the colony.

William Bird, father of Hopewell's founder, built Hopewell Forge in 1743. When he died in 1761, he had several thousand acres of land, three forges on Hay Creek, a furnace west of Reading, and a town house in Birdsboro. Eventually his son Mark acquired the Birdsboro forges. To supply cast iron for his forges, Mark Bird

built Hopewell Furnace in 1770. He recruited skilled workers from nearby Warwick and Reading furnaces. Bird built homes for the workers who moved to the furnace and operated a store where they could buy their necessities. He lived in the "Big House" near the furnace. A barn sheltered the horses that hauled the charcoal, ore, and limestone for the furnace, supplies for the village, and finished products to market. There were also a blacksmith shop and other utility buildings.

Hopewell Furnace served and was served by the country for miles around. Hopewell Village proper was the center of a large community. More than sixty-five people worked for the Furnace or supplied the people who did with meat, grain, flour, shoes, and other items.

The Furnace was hardly in production when the Revolutionary War started. Some cannon and shot were cast at the Furnace. Mark Bird saw service as a colonel in the militia and got desperately needed supplies to Washington's army at Valley Forge during the agonizing winter of 1778. After the Revolution, in 1786, Hopewell Furnace and the Birdsboro works were sold by the sheriff. During the next fourteen years the Furnace passed through a number of hands. In 1800 it was purchased by Matthew and Thomas Brooke, who turned it into a profitable venture by manufacturing stoves. In Hopewell Village stone houses replaced the earlier log houses, families put down roots, a school was built, and sons were trained for the expanding number of skilled jobs at the Furnace. As industry developed new and better iron-producing techniques, the iron industry became concentrated in the cities. Anthracite furnaces could be built in the cities and produce iron at a lower cost. The depression of 1841 forced Hopewell Furnace out of the stove business. In 1883, after 113 years of continuous operation, it "blow'd out" for the last time.

The federal government acquired the site of Hopewell Village in 1935. Many of the major structures had survived basically intact, and its significance as an early American industrial community was obvious. It now comprises 848 acres. The village roads are historic wagon roads. Just below the visitor center is the 1757 Valley Forge–Reading Road. One can view the charcoal shed and house where the charcoal was stored. There is a charcoal hearth, where it took about an acre of hardwood forest to make enough charcoal for one day's furnace operation. There is the water wheel and blast machinery, where the water from Hopewell Lake turns the wheel that operates the blast machinery. Teamsters dumped charcoal for spring-through-fall use under the connecting shed. There are other industrial structures to be viewed, including the Tuyere Arch, Cast Arch, and Bridge House. Near the furnace is the blacksmith shop, where wrought-iron tools and hardware were made for the community. The Tenant Houses number four of more than a dozen company houses once occupied by the furnace workers. There are the wagon scales where loads of castings were weighed. The Office-Store was the nerve-center of the Village; a clerk kept the records and sold nearly everything the workers needed. The spring house supplied the ironmaster and his family with drinking water. The bakeovens and the kitchen were used to feed the workers who ate in the big house. The ironmaster's house was occupied by either the owner or his manager.

HOPEWELL VILLAGE is five miles south of Birdsboro, Pennsylvania, and eight miles from the Morgantown Interchange of the Pennsylvania Turnpike. It is open daily from 9:30 A.M. to 5:30 P.M. except Christmas. From May 30 through Labor Day the site remains open until 7:30 P.M. on Saturdays, Sundays, and holidays. There are no admission charges listed in their literature.

John Dickinson was born November 2, 1732, at "Crosiadore," the estate of his parents, Samuel and Mary Cadwalader Dickinson, in Talbot County, Maryland. His father acquired large tracts of land in Kent County, Delaware, where he built a mansion and moved his family in January of 1740. There John was raised until 1750, when he went to Philadelphia to read law with John Morland. Then he studied at the Middle Temple in London until 1757, when he returned to Philadelphia to practice his profession. His interest in politics led to his election to the Delaware General Assembly in 1760. This was followed by election to the Pennsylvania Assembly from Philadelphia in 1762 and 1764. The next year he was a delegate from that state to the Colonial Congress.

He wrote practically all the important documents of the American Congress up to the Declaration of Independence and so earned the title "Penman of the Revolution." His famous *Letters Of A Farmer in Pennsylvania* written in 1768 and his *A Song For American Freedom* of the same year contributed greatly toward showing the colonists their rights as free men. Because of an ideological quarrel with the revolutionary faction of the Congress, he refrained from signing the Declaration of Independence.

Within a week of the proclamation of independence he marched as a colonel at the head of his Philadelphia brigade against the enemy, which threatened to invade New York and New Jersey. He resumed his role as "The Penman of the Revolution" by drafting the Articles of Confederation in 1778. In 1781 he was elected president (governor) of Delaware. He resigned in 1782 to accept the presidency of Pennsylvania. He subsequently served Delaware in various capacities and maintained an active interest in political affairs until his death on February 14, 1808.

The large, strongly constructed brick dwelling, laid in Flemish bond, was built by Samuel Dickinson to face to the south and to connect by a lane through his broad fields with the landing on the nearby St. Jones River, which provided easy access by water to Wilmington and Philadelphia. As the household grew, additions were made; the dining room wing was added in 1752 and the kitchen in 1754. Barns, sheds, slave quarters, and other out-buildings were added.

There were no major changes in the mansion until 1804, when a fire weakened the roof and destroyed much of the interior woodwork. This damage was repaired by John Dickinson but in a simpler manner than his father had built. Since that time and until it was acquired for preservation it has been inhabited by tenants of the Dickinsons, the Logans and subsequent owners.

This venerable dwelling is more than a fine example of lower Delaware eighteenth-century plantation architecture; it is an historic site giving an insight to the way of living of one of the eminent founders of our country. In 1952 it was purchased by the National Society of the Colonial Dames of America in the State of Delaware and presented to the state of Delaware. Following archaeological, architectural, and historical research, an advisory committee carried forward the restoration. Furnishings were added that were once owned by the family or are typical of the southeastern Pennsylvania–Delaware area. The gardens were recreated with the aid of a number of the garden clubs in the state.

The JOHN DICKINSON MANSION is located five miles east of Dover, Delaware, three miles east of Route 113 on Kitts Hummock Road. It is open to the public Tuesdays through Saturdays 10:00 A.M. to 5:00 P.M.; Sundays from 1:00 P.M. to 5:00 P.M. It is closed Mondays, Easter, Independence Day, Labor Day, Thanksgiving, Christmas, and New Year's. There is no admission charge.

THE JOHN DICKINSON MANSION

THE MORRIS-JUMEL MANSION

NEW YORK, NEW YORK

Located on the highest elevation of Manhattan is the Morris-Jumel Mansion. In the days of the Dutch the area was called Haarlem Heights. When the English took over, they changed it to Mount Morris, and after the Revolution it became and remained Washington Heights.

The plot of land on which the mansion is situated was originally deeded in 1700 to a Dutch farmer named Jan Kiersen. He left it to his daughter, Jannetje, the wife of Jacob Dyckman. They sold the property in 1763 to James Carroll, who sold it two years later to wealthy young Lt. Col. Roger Morris. The new owner came to America from England at the age of eighteen with a commission of captaincy in the British army. He was an aide-de-camp to General Braddock during the French and Indian War, during which he became a friend of George Washington. He was wounded in Braddock's defeat; while recuperating in New York he met and married the wealthy Mary Philipse, who, it is said, was at one time courted by George Washington.

A month later he purchased the commission of major and sailed to serve with Wolfe on his expedition against Quebec. After being promoted to Lieutenant Colonel of the Forty-Seventh Regiment, he sold his commission in 1764 and returned to settle down with "Polly." In the same year he took his seat as a member of the Executive Council of the Province of New York. In 1765 he erected his mansion on the former Kiersen-Dyckman-Carroll property and named it Mount Morris. In those days the house commanded the finest view of any on Manhattan Island.

There, with his wife and their four children, he lived the life of a typical British squire until the outbreak of the Revolution. Being a Tory and realizing that victory for the rebels would mean the dissolution of his estate, he fled to England at the beginning of hostilities and remained for two and a half years. His wife and children resided at Philipse Manor with her sister-in-law. Upon his return to New York in 1777, Col. Morris, at the instance of the British Government, was given the post of Inspector of the Claims of Refugees, which he retained until the peace treaty was signed in 1783. The entire Morris family then sailed to England, where they permanently settled.

During the Revolution Mount Morris was taken over by American troops, and General Heath and his staff were quartered there. After the disastrous Battle of Long Island, General Washington retreated to Haarlem Heights and made the place his headquarters. When he abandoned that position, the British moved in, and the mansion housed General Sir Henry Clinton and his officers. During the seven years the British occupied New York they also occupied Mount Morris. When peace was declared, the house and land were confiscated and sold by the Commission of Forfeiture.

It was sold and resold several times. It was renamed Calumet Hall, served for a time as a tavern, and was a stopping place for the stage coaches en route to Albany. An unknown farmer lived in it when General George Washington visited his old headquarters and entertained John Adams, Alexander Hamilton, Henry Knox, and their wives.

In 1810 Stephen Jumel and his wife became entranced with the old Morris Mansion and purchased it and thirty-five acres of land for $10,000. They energetically went about renovating and refurnishing it until it was one of the most beautiful homes in the country. They restored it in the style of the early nineteenth century, when the Federal influence was in fashion.

Stephen Jumel amassed a fortune as a wine merchant, and at his death in 1832 his wife became one of the richest women in America. A year later she married Aaron Burr, former Vice President of the United States. The marriage was of short duration and ended in separation. Mrs. Jumel died at the age of ninety-three in 1865.

The house once again passed through several ownerships until 1903, when it was purchased by the City of New York for $235,000; the custodianship was given to the Washington Headquarters Association, founded by the Daughters of the American Revolution. The house was again renovated and refurnished and the grounds relandscaped.

The Morris-Jumel Mansion is of the mid-Georgian period of architecture. The front façade has four columns, two stories in height, with a pediment at the top. This was unusual architecture for a prerevolutionary house. The house is built of brick encased in wood with quoined corners. The exterior is painted white. One of the postcolonial features added by the Jumels is the imposing front entrance doorway, with flanking sidelights and elliptical fanlight. They are filled with plain and amber-tinted glass. An ornamental balcony projects over the entrance under the portico.

In refurnishing it was necessary to consider the fact that two noted families of widely separated periods lived there. It necessitated combining the prerevolutionary Georgian period with those of the American Federal and French Empire. All the window draperies are authentic period patterns. The wide, arched central hall is furnished with late eighteenth- and early nineteenth-century pieces. At the left of the entrance is the small parlor or tea room, where the marriage ceremony of the Widow Jumel and Aaron Burr was performed in 1833, when the bride was fifty-eight and the groom seventy-eight.

Across the hall is the stately Georgian dining room, where many persons of fame assembled for elaborate dinner parties. The room is furnished in eighteenth-century mahogany furniture. At the rear of the hall is the large octagonal drawing room. The Morris family used it as a library; later it became General Washington's military headquarters, and four court martials were held here. The Jumels used it as a drawing room. Facing the stair-hall is the library that was used as a nursery for the Morris children. During the military occupancy it served as a guard's room. Among the pieces of furniture is a grandfather's clock once owned by Mrs. Jumel. The broad stairway leads to the spacious hall on the upper floor, which is furnished with personal belongings of the Jumels. The southeast bedroom belonged to Mrs. Jumel and is furnished in the neoclassic elegance of the Empire period with the original Jumel bed and chairs. The room across the hall was occupied by Aaron Burr and contains his desk, trunk, and portrait. The northwest bedroom contains furniture owned by the Jumels, including a four-poster bed. The suite of three rooms over the drawing room was the private quarters of General Washington. The rear room is where he slept and wrote his dispatches and planned his military maneuvers. The third floor was probably used as extra guest chambers, since the servants' quarters were located in the basement with the kitchen.

The MORRIS-JUMEL MANSION is located on West 160th Street and Edgecomb Avenue in the Washington Heights section of New York City. It is open every day except Monday from 11:00 A.M. to 5:00 P.M. Admission is free.

Marlpit Hall, the Taylor Homestead, was built in stages beginning in 1684. The house then consisted of a kitchen with stairs to a room above. The large original beams and the fireplace are still to be seen. The remainder of the house was added in the early eighteenth century. Edmund Taylor, the original founder of Marlpit Hall, was born in Shadoxhurst, Kent, England, the son of John Taylor. He migrated from London to America; he stopped in Rhode Island but settled in Middletown, New Jersey, where he built Marlpit Hall.

The house contains seventeenth- and eighteenth-century furniture, much of it from the collection of Early American furniture of Mrs. J. Amory Haskell, who is also responsible for saving the house from demolition. The kitchen, with its original fireplace, features seventeenth- and early eighteenth-century furniture and cooking utensils. The parlor, part of the newer addition to the house added in the early eighteenth century, displays furniture of the early eighteenth century and appointments and furnishings from the Taylor family and other Monmouth County families. Notable features of the eighteenth-century additions to Marlpit Hall are the original paneling, dented trim, corner cupboard, corner fireplace, and the huge front door.

MARLPIT HALL is now owned and maintained by the Monmouth County Historical Association. It is located at 137 Kings Highway in Middletown, New Jersey. It is open from 11:00 A.M. to 5:00 P.M. Tuesday, Thursday, and Saturday and from 2:00 P.M. to 5:00 P.M. on Sunday. It is closed during January. There is no admission charge.

MARLPIT HALL

Marlpit Hall, 1684   *Middletown, New Jerse*

Located in the City of New Castle, a modern and busy small city that retains a fascinating and visible link with America's earliest years, Old Court House is the original colonial capitol and America's oldest state house. The story of Old Court House began almost a half a century before the thirteen colonies declared themselves independent.

In 1732 only the central part of today's Court House existed. It had replaced an earlier courthouse built sometime between 1682 and 1689 and destroyed by fire in 1729. The roof lines of the original central wing and the cupola were different from what we see today, but, generally, it is the same building. The Old Court House was used as a state house. Delegates of the people of the three counties on the Delaware took steps toward the formation of the Delaware State at the request of the Continental Congress. In that building Delaware's first Constitution was adopted. There also the Delaware Assembly approved the Declaration of Independence, and Delaware's first president was chosen by the Council and Assembly of the new state.

The importance of the building grew, and in 1765 two small wings were added east and west of the central section; for years this was the stage on which moved the deadliners of stirring drama in which a new nation was formed. Even when the capital of Delaware was moved from New Castle to Dover, the Court House continued to be the focal point of the orderly processes of government under the federal constitution and the laws of the state. An addition was made in 1802 to the east wing that placed that section substantially in its present state. The small west wing of 1765 was torn down in 1845 and replaced with the present west wing, primarily to house county records.

The structure was the hub of the county's government through the formative years of the nation and on into the nineteenth century until 1881, when the county seat was transferred to Wilmington. The old building was allowed to deteriorate slowly. Many architectural changes were made, destroying the original beauty of the building. The brick was covered with stucco. The interior was cut up into rooms. False tin ceilings were put over the old beams. It became a drill hall, a meeting hall, a tea room.

With state funds and private gifts, restoration of the main building has recently been completed. All the architectural work is as faithful to the original as available records permit, and some portions of the original construction remain intact. The two hand-turned long-leaf yellow pine columns supporting the main beam of the ceiling stand as they did 230 years ago. The courtroom is finished in authentic colonial decor. It is an excellent example of architecturally accurate renovation.

OLD COURT HOUSE is in the center of a portion of New Castle preserved as an authentic historic shrine. It is bounded by the riverfront on the east, Fourth Street on the west, and Harmony and Delaware Streets on the north and south. It is open daily from 11:00 A.M. to 4:00 P.M. It is closed all day Wednesday. There are no admission fees listed in the literature.

COMBINATION SEAT DESK, OLD BARRACKS

The Old Barracks stands as a unique memorial to the late colonial and revolutionary history of America. Erected in 1758 on what are now the State House grounds in Trenton, this beautiful U-shaped stone building had to be rescued from obscurity and restored by a militant and enlightened few. The ownership is now vested in the State of New Jersey, thus insuring its permanence and support.

The Old Barracks was built during the French and Indian War to prevent the forcible billeting of British soldiers on private householders. The situation had become so intolerable in the winters, when troops were withdrawn from the frontiers to the towns, that the General Assembly recommended the erection of five barracks for winter quarters for 1500 men. The Old Barracks is the only one that survives. Constructed from native undressed stone, the structure was two stories high with a narrow balcony running the length of the second story. The first troops, the Inniskilling Regiment of Foot, composed mainly of Irishmen, occupied the building in December, 1758.

Soldiers and officers used the Barracks during the winter months until the close of the war between England and France in May, 1763, when British forces were no longer needed in the colony. The Barracks Master was ordered to sell the furnishings and rent the buildings. The outbreak of the Revolution brought the Trenton Barracks back to its original purpose. It was variously occupied by British troops, Hessian mercenaries, and American soldiers, depending on who had control of the territory. The Battle of Trenton was fought not far from its doors in

the early morning hours of December 26, 1776. The Barracks was also used as a hospital for wounded American soldiers; six hundred were brought in after the Battle of Yorktown in November, 1781.

After the close of the Revolution the Barracks was sold, and the building was divided into private dwellings. In 1855 the southern L-shaped section was purchased as a home for aged and widowed women. In 1899 it was sold to a group of women who organized to prevent the Barracks being demolished. In 1902 that same group formed the Old Barracks Association to preserve and restore their purchase. They maintained it as a small museum for ten years. They persuaded the State of New Jersey to buy the northern wing and the restoration of the building in its entirety was in sight.

The restoration was completed in 1917 and has since been welcoming visitors from all over the world. Noteworthy in its exhibits are furniture, silver, and china of the colonial and federal periods, many pieces associated with important people in New Jersey history. There are mementos of George Washington and an officer's coatee that belonged to Colonel Rall, commander of a Hessian Regiment at the Battle of Trenton. An excellent collection of firearms shows a blunderbuss, a huge duck gun, early muskets, and Committee of Safety and Charleville rifles. Dioramas illustrate both the Battle of Trenton and the interior appearance of the Barracks when it housed British troops two centuries ago.

The OLD BARRACKS is located on South Willow Street in Trenton, New Jersey, near the State Capitol. It is open weekdays May through August from 10:00 A.M. to 5:00 P.M. and weekdays September through April from 10:00 A.M. to 4:00 P.M. It is open Sundays all year from 2:00 P.M. to 5:00 P.M. It is closed Thanksgiving Day, Christmas Day, New Year's Day, and Washington's Birthday. Admission for adults is twenty-five cents, for children ten cents.

TRIUMPHAL ARCH, OLD BARRACKS

D.A.R. ROOM, OLD BARRACKS

MONROE, NEW YORK

Located in the historically rich mid-Hudson Valley area is the recreation of a typical village of a century ago. Fascinated by the story of invention, adaptation, variation, and improvement shown by the tools of our ancestors, Mr. Roscoe Smith, a local industrialist, collected what he called "the tools that built America." Along with these he collected glass, china, costumes, and other artifacts used by the "average" American of one hundred years ago. Over the years the collection grew to such proportions that it became necessary to properly house it. In 1950 the doors of Old Museum Village opened. Since that time it has grown from fourteen to more than thirty-five buildings. These buildings are modern recreations.

Beginning with the log cabin home, the first

building in the making of a pioneer community, and ending with the most modern of the group, the Vernon Apothecary Shop, the many buildings of this crossroad village trace the growth of a village from the Age of Homespun to the Age of Industry.

The Log Cabin, contrary to common opinion, was not a spontaneous innovation but was a tried and successful form of construction brought to America by the Swedes who settled along the Delaware. Within the confines of this small dwelling of the eighteenth century most functions of everyday life were performed. Because of the need to preserve space, furniture was constructed to serve more than one function. This cabin was moved to Smith's Clove from the West Point area.

OLD

The Byron Kellam Blacksmith Shop is the very hub of the Village. There all the tools and utensils of the community were made and the horses and oxen shod. In this blacksmith shop visitors may assist the blacksmith.

The William Gaunt Wagonmaking Shop is appropriately right next door to the blacksmith shop. In cooperation with the blacksmith, the building of wagons and carriages was carried out.

In a day when people walked a great deal, the Bootmaking Shop was assured a living keeping shoes and boots in repair and replacing them when necessary.

Belknap and McCann, Candlemakers made scented toilet soap as well as fulling and brown oil soap for cleaning rugs, hats, and so on.

Candles were made in molds of tin, pewter, and pottery. Tallow was purchased from local farmers in the form of animal fats. You can watch candlemaking demonstrated in this candle shop.

Smith's Clove Schoolhouse is a reconstruction of a school that stood in Monroe in 1805. At that time the school day was usually from 7 A.M. to 4 P.M. with a longer period of vacation, which allowed the children to be home during the warmer months to help with the planting, cultivating, and harvesting of the crops. You can see the old blackboard, globe, maps, and a cat-of-nine-tales for discipline.

The J. S. Gregory Saddle, Harness and Trunkmaker's Shop provided the villagers with equipment for their horses, and the Hulse Tinshop supplied the housewife with breadpans, cookie

MUSEUM VILLAGE OF SMITH'S CLOVE

cutters, pudding and ice cream molds, milk pans, milk pails, strainers, dippers, and the like. The well-known Gillian Bailey collection of tinware is displayed here.

Smith's Clove Broom Company made not only brooms but also slat baskets and woven chairs in rush or hickory slat. Broommaking was one of the first crafts to take on almost factory proportions. Broommaking is demonstrated on the early equipment in the Broom Company.

The Benjamin Barry Cooperage was responsible for all the casks and barrels necessary for the village and also butter churns, tubs, pails and measures.

The Smith's Clove Cider Mill had the pleasant task of making cider from the freshly picked apples in the autumn. Often the mill operator ran some of this cider through a still to make apple whiskey, commonly called Applejack.

Smith's Clove Hose House is the fire house. It is equipped with an 1820 Washington Hand Pumper and a Poughkeepsie Pumper plus plenty of brass hose and leather hose. There is also the hand-drawn Hose Cart and a Ladder Pole. The Bell Tower atop the hose house served as a watch tower for spotting fires.

The J. C. Merritt General Store has all the necessities, fancies, and conceits that enthralled our ancestors. There you will find the familiar cracker barrel, pot-bellied stove, and checker board. There also was the village Post Office and the village social center, where the politics and problems of the day were discussed while one purchased the many items in the store.

The Charles Vernon Apothecary Shop served as a doctor's office as well. The local druggist was consulted by his customers, and he would diagnose their ailments and prescribe and compound the cure. There are his herbs and chemicals, his mortar and pestle, and pill-making machine.

The OLD MUSEUM VILLAGE can be reached from the New York Thruway Exit 16 at Harriman, west on Route 6 and 17 (Quickway), 4½ miles to Exit 129, Museum Village Road. It is open from April 15 to October 31, 10:00 A.M. to 5:00 P.M. From June 15 through Labor Day it is open from 10:00 A.M. to 6:00 P.M. Admission for adults is $1.50, children sixty cents.

VERNON APOTHECARY, SMITH'S COVE

The restored home of Pennsylvania's only Chief Executive, James Buchanan, who was President of the United States from 1857 to 1861, is on the western edge of the city of Lancaster, halfway between Philadelphia and Gettysburg, in the heart of the storied Pennsylvania Dutch country. Named Wheatland by its first occupant, a Lancaster banker, the home was built in 1828 amid acres of wheat fields, which gave the building its title. Ownership of the home changed hands in 1845 when William Meredith of Philadelphia, a legislator, jurist, and later Secretary of the Treasury, purchased it for his use as a summer home. Buchanan bought the home from Meredith in 1848 for $6,750 while serving as Secretary of State in the cabinet of James K. Polk, eleventh President of the United States.

Situated atop a gently rising slope, Wheatland bears a dignified stately appearance often likened to the southern mansions of the same period. Structurally, Wheatland gives visitors the impression of a building erected in three separate stages. The two-story main portion of the building is square and is flanked by two three-story wings set back from the central structure. The French influence on eighteenth-century architecture is hinted at by the front porch, which is reached by stairs on all three sides. The main entrance is framed by four white pillars reminiscent of the Old South.

Buchanan was the nation's only bachelor president, and Wheatland never had more than four permanent occupants: himself, his fabled niece Harriet Lane, who was official hostess during Buchanan's administration, James Buchanan Henry, a nephew who was his private secretary, and Hetty Parker, a housekeeper. Buchanan's life provides an interesting study of personal triumphs and tragedies, most of which are reflected by Wheatland.

Born of a family of average means in 1791 in Franklin County, Pennsylvania, Buchanan's family moved to Lancaster shortly after the turn of the century; he soon became a promising young lawyer. He became engaged to a local belle, Anne Coleman, in 1819, but her millionaire ironmaster father disapproved of the projected marriage. Anne died in December of that year, reportedly of tuberculosis. Historians point to Anne's untimely death as being responsible for

Buchanan's decision to bury himself in public life. He placed Anne's portrait on a wall of his bedroom at Wheatland, where it is today.

After serving several terms in the House of Representatives, Buchanan was appointed ambassador to Russia in 1832. He was elected to the U.S. Senate two years later and was minister to the Court of St. James following his term as Polk's Secretary of State. He was nominated for the presidency in 1856 at the age of sixty-five and was elected the fifteenth President after his famed "front porch campaign" at Wheatland. He assumed executive control of a nation already divided in sentiment over the slavery question. His attempts at unification proved to be futile, and he left the White House in 1861 broken by his failure to prevent the forthcoming Civil War and saddened by the public's indignation.

At Wheatland there are numerous mementos of the government positions held by Buchanan, including signed portraits of Queen Victoria, Prince Albert, and the Prince of Wales in the drawing room. There is the rare and priceless "Emperor's Bowl" presented to Buchanan by the Mikado in 1860. It is thirty-seven inches in diameter, twenty-two inches in height, and beautifully decorated with the "Three Friends of Winter" by one of Japan's greatest designers.

The mansion contains much of Buchanan's furniture, china, and silver. One of the interesting pieces in the parlor is Harriet Lane's Chickering piano, which was given to her by her uncle in 1857. Buchanan's study, with his original furniture, is arranged as in his day. It was there that many affairs of state were settled. The bedrooms and guest rooms on the second floor look as though they are ready for the President's return from Washington. Visitors are conducted through the various rooms by guides in period costumes.

WHEATLAND is located on Marietta Avenue near President Avenue in the city of Lancaster. It is open from March 15 through November 30 daily from 9:00 A.M. to 5:00 P.M. and on Sundays from 10:00 A.M. to 5:00 P.M. Admission is seventy-five cents, children under twelve free.

LIBRARY, WHEATLAND

Practically unchanged architecturally since it was built more than 160 years ago, and surprisingly untouched by deterioration, Rock Ford is an authentic example of refined country living during the United States' first formative years.

General Edward Hand was born in 1744 in the Province of Leinster, Ireland. After medical training at Trinity College, Dublin, he emigrated to America in 1767 with the Eighteenth Royal Irish Regiment of Foot. Resigning from the British service in 1774, Hand came to Lancaster to practice medicine and surgery. On July 22, 1775, he began duty leading troops as a lieutenant colonel in William Thompson's Pennsylvania Rifle Battalion. Between then and his honorable discharge as a major general in 1800 he saw service at the Battle of Trenton, the

Battle of Long Island, the Battle of White Plains, the Battle of Princeton, the campaign against the Iroquois, and the Surrender at Yorktown. He served on the tribunal that convicted Major John André after the exposure of Benedict Arnold's plan to surrender West Point. He became the Army's Adjutant General and was highly regarded by George Washington, who later visited him at Lancaster.

After the war Hand was a member of the Continental Congress and the Assembly of Pennsylvania and Chief Burgess of Lancaster. Upon construction of the house, he moved to Rock Ford in 1793 and died there on September 3, 1802.

Rock Ford is a brick mansion of sturdy Georgian style and simple, pleasing design. It is

situated four miles south of Lancaster's Penn Square, commanding a fine view of the Conestoga River. Pleasantly spacious, Rock Ford's four floors are all built on the center hall and four corner rooms plan so typical of the period. Original eighteenth-century floors, stair-treads and rails, shutters, doors, cupboards, paneling, and even window glass greet the visitor. Swatches of original wall paints—of surprisingly bold colors—are visible for comparison.

The discovery of the inventory of General Hand's estate has permitted the location of articles that were in the house during Hand's time. Archaeological diggings have produced important artifacts preserved over the generations by eroded soil piled six or more feet deep around the homestead. In addition, foundations of out-buildings mentioned in early tax lists—such as a wood shed, ice house, smoke house, and spring house—have been uncovered.

Still yielding the secrets of its past to researchers, Rock Ford is a preserved, rather than restored house, where visitors can see and touch the same structural elements that existed in the glorious days of the early republic.

ROCK FORD is located within the Lancaster City Limits bordering Williamson Park, at the junction of South Duke Street and the Conestoga River, along Rock Ford Road. It is open to the public each weekday from 10:00 A.M. to 5:00 P.M. and on Sundays from noon to 5:00 P.M. Adult admission is seventy-five cents, children twenty-five cents.

ROCK FORD

ROCK FORD
LANCASTER, PA.
GROUNDS RESTORATION

When Theodore Roosevelt was fifteen, his father established the family's summer residence at Oyster Bay, and the boy spent his vacations exploring the woods and fields on Cove Neck. Six months after graduating from Harvard young Roosevelt bought the hill on Cove Neck where Sagamore Hill now stands.

Some time after, just before a final agreement was signed with a New York firm of architects to build a home on the site, Theodore Roosevelt's wife and mother died in the same house on the same day. Determined to have a suitable home for his infant daughter, he commissioned a Long Island architect to build the rambling, twenty-two-room Victorian structure of frame and brick that became known as Sagamore Hill. It was named for the old Sagamore Mohannis, who, as chief of his little tribe, signed away his rights to the land.

The young squire of Sagamore Hill was named a member of the U. S. Civil Service Commission—his first major step in public service. Then he became president of the Police Commission of the City of New York, Assistant Secretary of the Navy, lieutenant colonel of the famed Rough Riders, governor of New York, Vice President, and finally Chief Executive. It was on the wide piazza of Sagamore Hill that Roosevelt was formally notified of his nomination as governor of New York in 1898, as Vice President in 1900, and as President in 1904.

Not only was Sagamore Hill the center of the day-to-day administration of the country's affairs during the summers from 1901 to 1909, but it also saw numerous dramatic events of national and international importance. For more than thirty years Sagamore Hill was one of the most conspicuous homes in America, talked about all over the United States. The doings of the Roosevelts and their kin at the "Summer White House" filled reams of newspaper copy.

Today it is little changed from the time, a half century ago, when it was the home of a distinguished American. On the first floor are a large center hall, the library that served as Theodore Roosevelt's private office, the dining room, Mrs. Roosevelt's drawing room, the kitchen, and the spacious north or Trophy Room, which was designed by Roosevelt's friend C. Grant LaFarge, son of the artist John LaFarge. The thirty-by-forty-foot room is built of Philippine and American woods and is crammed with trophies from his hunting expeditions, books, paintings, flags. It best reflects the spirit of Theodore Roosevelt.

The second floor contains the family bedrooms, the nursery, guest rooms, and the room with the great porcelain bathtub.

The Gun Room, housing Roosevelt's large collection of hunting arms, is on the top floor. He sometimes went there to write or to entertain his friends away from the bustle of the household. Other rooms, once servants' quarters, contain memorabilia relating to the President, his wife, and his children.

Furnishings throughout the house are original Roosevelt pieces. In every room are items used and loved by the family. On every hand are crowded bookshelves, the contents revealing the wide range of Roosevelt's interests. On the south and west side of the house is the spacious piazza from which Roosevelt looked out over Oyster Bay and Long Island Sound. On the grounds are landscaped gardens and the small animal cemetery where the family's beloved pets were buried.

SAGAMORE HILL is located at the end of Cove Neck Road, Oyster Bay, Long Island, New York. It is open from 10:00 A.M. to 5:00 P.M. every day except Tuesdays, Thanksgiving Day, Christmas Day, and New Year's Day. Admission is fifty cents.

MASTER BEDROOM, SAGAMORE HILL

ANCIENT KITCHEN, SHERWOOD HOUSE

Historic Sherwood House is one of the relatively few prerevolutionary houses still standing in the New York metropolitan area. It was built about 1740 by Thomas Sherwood, farmer, constable, and collector of the town of Yonkers, on land leased from Frederick Philipse, whose vast Manor extended from Spuyten Duyvil to the Croton River.

Stephen Sherwood, son of Thomas, bought the farm from the Commissioners of Forfeiture in 1785 after the Revolution. In 1801 the place was purchased by Dr. John Ingersoll, Yonkers' first physician, who lived there until his death in 1827.

For nearly a century, from 1834 to 1923, the homestead was owned by Frederick Weed and his descendants. After serving as a tavern for some years, the old house was acquired by Consolidated Edison as part of a power-line right-of-way. The house and outbuildings were given to the Yonkers Historical Society, and the land on which they stand was leased to the Society so that the buildings might be restored and preserved.

Sherwood House is a fine example of the Hudson Valley colonial farmhouse. It is literally built into a steep hillside, with basement of native stone and upper stories of wide clapboards. The two-story porch is an interesting feature, the curve of its roof suggesting regional Dutch influence.

After more than two centuries of continuous occupancy this sturdy structure stands today in virtually its original form. The huge kitchen fireplace with its smoke-stained lintel and "beehive" bakeoven is intact. The interior walls of the house, covered with primitive mud plaster, have stood well the wear and tear of time. The hand-hewn beams and rafters, joined by wooden pegs, are reminders of construction methods of long ago. Interesting too are the hand-wrought hinges and latches, divided Dutch doors, and small-paned windows. These and many other details bear witness to the antiquity of the house and make it a place of architectural as well as historical interest.

The rooms have been furnished with antiques that reflect the decorative periods and tastes of its various occupants.

SHERWOOD HOUSE is located on the south side of Tuckahoe Road at its intersection with the Sprain Brook Parkway in Yonkers, New York. It is open on Saturday, Sunday, and holiday afternoons from 2:00 P.M. to 5:00 P.M. from mid-May to mid-October. Admission is fifty cents, children twenty-five cents.

GERMANTOWN, PHILADELPHIA, PENNSYLVANIA

James Logan, the builder of Stenton, came to Philadelphia in 1699 at the age of twenty-five. He had been appointed secretary to William Penn, who in 1682 was granted the Charter of Pennsylvania. In 1701, when William Penn returned to England, Logan was appointed attorney for the proprietors and so continued until his death. In 1714 he married Sarah Read of Philadelphia. In 1715 he was commissioned justice of the Common Pleas and in 1723 became presiding judge and mayor of Philadelphia. From 1702 to 1747 he was a member of the Provincial Council and eventually its president. The climax to his career occurred when he became chief justice of Pennsylvania. On his death in 1751 he left 2,000 volumes to the city of Philadelphia, the basis of the noted Loganian Library.

William Logan, eldest surviving son, succeeded his father as attorney for the Penn family. He devoted himself mainly to agriculture and the welfare of the North American Indians. In 1740 he married Hannah Emlen. In 1743 he was elected to the Common Council of Philadelphia. From 1747 to 1776 he was a member of the Provincial Council. He died in 1776.

Dr. George Logan, second son of William, inherited Stenton from his father. Educated in England, he received his medical degree from the University of Edinburgh in 1779. In 1781 he married Deborah Norris. Her writings give a vivid picture of the great and famous who were Stenton's constant guests. George Logan devoted himself to medicine and agriculture. He was elected to the Pennsylvania Assembly eight times and became a United States senator in 1800. He was prominent as an agriculturist and wrote extensively on the subject. He died in 1821.

During the Revolution General Washington occupied Stenton on August 23, 1777, and General Sir William Howe made it his headquarters, from which he directed the Battle of Germantown.

Stenton was continuously occupied by the Logan family for six generations. In 1900 it became the property of the City of Philadelphia and in 1910 was given into the custody of the Pennsylvania Society, Colonial Dames of America.

Stenton Mansion is of brick, in the then current mode of England. It is devoid of ornamentation. The beautiful restraint of early Pennsylvania architecture, influenced by the guiding principle of the Friends simplicity, is everywhere apparent at Stenton. The interior contains excellent paneling, doorways and stairs. The stairs are rather massive in scale in harmony with the early date of their erection. In Logan's time it was a favorite sleeping place of Indian visitors. The entrance hall is laid with English brick in diagonal lines, and the wall is paneled to the ceiling. A handsome arch with double doors, also arched, leads to the stair hall. Excellently paneled parlors are on either side of the hall and are entered through folding doors.

Across the front of the second story extend two notable rooms, which comprised one of the most famous libraries of the colonies—James Logan's library of more than 3,000 volumes. Stenton possesses two secret passages and a stairway—a "whispering closet"—off the main hall, and an underground passage leads to the barn. At the back there is still the family burying ground. There lies Dinah, the slave caretaker, whose quick wit saved Stenton when it was ordered burned by the British.

STENTON MANSION is located at 18th and Courtland Streets in the Germantown area of Philadelphia. It is open to the public Tuesday through Saturday from 1:00 P.M. to 5:00 P.M. Admission is twenty-five cents.

WASHINGTON IRVING'S HOME

In 1835 Washington Irving purchased a small estate along the Hudson River about twenty-five miles north of Manhattan on the border line of the present-day village of Tarrytown and Irvington. The house that stood on the property was built in the late seventeenth century in the typical Dutch country architecture of that time. In the eighteenth century it was owned by a branch of the Van Tassel family, immortalized by Irving in the character Katrina Van Tassel in his *Legend of Sleepy Hollow*.

Between 1835 and 1837 Irving remodeled and enlarged the small dwelling that was eventually to house, at various times, his large family of nieces, nephews, and brothers. The house began to take on the appearance of the retreat of a romantic gentleman of the nineteenth century. Its situation was on a bank high above the Hudson River. The architectural style was personal to Irving. The Dutch stepped gables surmounted by ancient weathervanes were combined with architectural details from many of the revival styles popular in that day.

Irving purchased Sunnyside both as a retreat from the busy literary and social world in which he had taken such an active part, and for the greater economy of country living. Washington Irving was not only America's first internationally known man of letters but also a diplomat who served in Spain and England and was one of America's first ambassadors of good will in Europe. He knew all the important painters, writers and intellectuals of his day in the United States, England, and on the Continent.

Irving's study was the focal point for visitors to Sunnyside in his day. The commodious walnut desk was presented to him by his publisher, G. P. Putnam. The daybed in the draped alcove (as shown in the drawing by Irving's friend, the architect Alexander Jackson Davis) was used nightly by Irving for the first ten years of his life at Sunnyside, because his relatives and friends filled all the other rooms. The books in the study are all a part of Irving's own library. The parlor, with its square rosewood piano and beautiful view of the river from its windows was the center of family life. All the pictures hanging in the small gallery belonged to Irving. The iron cooking range and the iron sink with running water in the kitchen were installed late in Irving's life.

Upstairs the visitor is instantly struck by the unique arrangement and interior architecture of the rooms. Irving devised sloping barrel ceilings and ingenious arches, which were incorporated into a pleasing whole. The room in which Irving died is located in the southwest corner. It contains a tester Sheraton bed and a number of his personal effects. The guest room contains two arched alcoves and is furnished with painted cottage furniture. Farther down the hall are the rooms occupied by Irving's brother Ebenezer and his two nieces. Ebenezer's room is furnished in a spartan manner. The furniture in it was undoubtedly made by the local cabinetmaker. The nieces' room strikes a note of gaiety with its floral-patterned carpet, large mahogany sleigh bed, chest of drawers, and sewing stands—all typical of the furnishings of the room of a fashionable lady of that day. A guest room at the rear of the upstairs contains a remarkable cast iron bed, probably made at one of the foundries along the Hudson.

In 1847 Irving had a three-story tower built, which was referred to as the Pagoda. This area contains four rooms, which were occupied by household servants and sometimes by overflow guests. The kitchen yard at the rear of the house has been carefully restored from documentary sources. A root cellar for storing vegetables, meat and milk occupies two floors. The woodshed was used for storing the kitchen and fireplace wood, and an ice house was used for the summer storage of ice. There are lovely walks on the property and a delightful waterfall.

Irving was at Sunnyside working on his monumental *Life of Washington* when he died in 1859.

SUUNYSIDE is on Route 9 in Westchester County, New York. It is open Monday through Friday, April 1 through November 15, from 10:00 A.M. to 5:00 P.M. and November 16 through March 31 from 12:00 noon to 4:00 P.M. On Saturdays and Sundays it is open from 10:00 A.M. to 5:00 P.M. It is closed on Thanksgiving Day, Christmas Day, and New Year's Day. Admission is $1.00, children 6–14, fifty cents.

SHERWOOD-JAYNE HOUSE

EAST SETAUKET, NEW YORK

William Jayne, a chaplain in Cromwell's army, came to America about 1670. His son probably built this house about 1730, the east end of the main structure perhaps being added about 1790. Mr. Howard C. Sherwood, a founder of the Society for the Preservation of Long Island Antiquities, bought the house and added and altered many of the original features to make the building livable in the modern world. Thus, the wing and other later protrusions on the rear provided more living area and space for modern utilities and now afford quarters for the caretaker.

The main house is furnished with Mr. Sherwood's varied collection of antiques; early furniture, paintings, lighting devices, pewter, ceramics, textiles, and other items effect a reconciliation of today's living with the past. Set in a charming rural setting with sheep grazing in the pasture, this "saltbox" house boasts such features as decorative wall paintings in the east parlor and east bedroom, rarities on Long Island. The paneling in the west parlor is from an old East Setauket parsonage; that in the room above came from an early Manhattan house.

The SHERWOOD-JAYNE HOUSE is located on Old Post Road in East Setauket, Long Island, New York. It can be reached by the North Country Road (Route 25A). It is open from May 29 to October 13, Monday, Wednesday, Thursday, and Friday from 1:00 P.M. to 5:00 P.M. Admission is fifty cents, children twenty-five cents.

THE THOMPSON HOUSE

SETAUKET, NEW YORK

This "saltbox" house, perhaps built in two or three stages, was begun about 1700, and the wings were added some years later. Occupied for about 178 years by the Thompson family, it was the birthplace in 1784 of Benjamin F. Thompson, Long Island historian. The main house reflects the character of the late seventeenth century, while certain details suggest the early eighteenth century. Interesting architectural features include the unusually high ceilings, heavy exposed framing, great fireplaces with unusual smoke channels, and early paneling.

Among the interesting things to see in the house are a quilt made from the wedding dress of Benjamin F. Thompson's mother, Long Island chairs, a folding press bed, linen and blankets made from flax and wool grown nearby, and excellent examples of early lighting devices, kitchen utensils, pewter, and ceramics of the period. One room is equipped with the tools and materials for spinning, dyeing, and other home crafts. Outdoors, the well-sweep is set off by a lovely little garden of culinary, medicinal, and fragrant herbs.

The THOMPSON HOUSE is located on North Country Road (25A) in Setauket. It is open from May 29 to October 13, Monday, Wednesday, Thursday, Friday, and Saturday from 1:00 P.M. to 5:00 P.M. It is open on Sunday from 2:00 P.M. to 6:00 P.M. Admission is fifty cents, children twenty-five cents.

CROTON-ON-HUDSON, NEW YORK

Van Cortlandt Manor reflects the way of life of a famous Hudson Valley family prominent in eighteenth-century agriculture, business, and politics. The Manor House was owned by the Van Cortlandt family from the seventeenth century until the middle of the 1940s.

Stephanus van Cortlandt, eldest son of Oloffe Stevense van Cortlandt, progenitor of this Dutch family in America, was a leading citizen of New York Province. He served on the governor's privy council for eight years. He was a judge in Admiralty, secretary of the Province, and chief justice of the Supreme Court. Between November 16, 1677, and June 17, 1697, he purchased more than 86,000 acres of land bounded by the Croton River on the south, Putnam County on the north, the Hudson River on the west and the Connecticut boundary on the east. This tract was erected into the Manor of Cortlandt by William III on June 17, 1697. He improved his property slowly. By 1718 the Manor listed only ninety-one inhabitants. The manor house was occupied only occasionally for fur trading, collecting manor rents, hunting, and fishing. On his death in 1700 the Croton Manor House and adjoining lands passed to his seventh child, Philip van Cortlandt (1683–1748). On the death of Philip the house passed to his eldest surviving son, Pierre van Cortlandt (1721–1814).

On inheriting Croton Manor House, Pierre enlarged the property and moved there with his wife and child in 1749. From this time, the van Cortlandt family made the house their permanent residence until the mid 1940s. Pierre and Joanna van Cortlandt lived a gracious country life at Croton. Their guests were many. By blood and marriage they were related to the great Hudson Valley families: The Philipses, Van Rensselaers, Schuylers, Livingstons, DePeysters, Clintons, DeLanceys. National figures —Benjamin Franklin, Governor Tryon, George Whitfield, John Jay, Rochambeau, DeKalb, Von Steuben, George and DeWitt Clinton—all visited here.

In addition to the problems of developing the manor lands, Pierre found time to represent Cortlandt Manor in the New York Assembly from 1768 to 1775. In 1775 he became a leading patriot and was one of the ratifiers of the Declaration of Independence. In May, 1776, he was appointed president of the Council of Safety. In 1777 he became the first lieutenant governor of the new state, a position he held until 1795.

During the revolutionary war years the house, on neutral ground, suffered pillage and structural damage. In 1785 the house was restored to its prewar appearance. The present restoration has returned it to its appearance at the time when it was most clearly identified with great people and events.

Since its enlargement in 1749, the Manor House has had the appearance of a comfortable Hudson Valley farmhouse. Its attractiveness lies in its simplicity of design, both inside and out. It contrasts favorably with equivalent Hudson Valley Manor houses built during the mid-eighteenth century. The lower floor contains the old family parlor, the kitchen, and the milk room. Built back in the hillside, these rooms are unquestionably a part of the original house on this site. The main floor contains the parlor, dining room, and bedchambers. The main floor rooms date from the enlargement of 1749. Most of the furnishings of the restored house are van Cortlandt family items originally in this structure. These date from the seventeenth century to the early nineteenth century and illustrate the Hudson Valley Dutch habit of carefully preserving and using inherited family pieces from generation to generation, rather than furnishing in any one particular period style.

The garden along the long walk was begun in 1749 by Joanna van Cortlandt when she planted white Scottish roses and yellow poppies brought from her childhood home. Successive generations of van Cortlandts developed the gardens in the manner seen today. This garden, carefully restored, repeats its eighteenth-century pattern.

From its beginning in 1723 and until a permanent bridge was built in 1819, the van Cortlandt Ferry was the only means of crossing the Croton River for travelers on the Albany Post Road. The ferry, a flat-bottomed scow pulled by a rope, was leased to tenants of the Van Cortlandt family. By law it was necessary for the ferry operator to provide a structure where travelers could rest, eat, and stable their horses. The Ferry House or tavern was such a structure. An architectural survey showed no evidence of a kitchen. Foundations found to the west, however, contained traces of a great brick fireplace. A separate kitchen was therefore constructed on these late-seventeenth-century foundations. The presence of a separate kitchen structure is extremely unusual in the eighteenth-century Hudson Valley.

Van Cortlandt Manor House was purchased by the late John D. Rockefeller Jr. in 1953. In 1954 and 1955 additional land was acquired, including the ferry house. Still later, more than 150 additional acres were added for the future protection of the property. In 1954 a five-year period of restoration began with an extensive research and building program under the direction of Colonial Williamsburg. The restored property was opened to the public in June, 1959.

VAN CORTLANDT MANOR is on Route 9 in Westchester County, near Croton-on-Hudson. It is open from Monday through Friday, April 1 through November 15, from 10:00 A.M. to 5:00 P.M. From November 16 through March 31 it is open from 12:00 noon to 4:00 P.M. On Saturdays and Sundays it is open from 10:00 A.M. to 5:00 P.M. It is closed on Thanksgiving Day, Christmas Day, and New Year's Day. Admission is $1.00, children 6–14, fifty cents.

VILLA BOSCOBEL

GARRISON-ON-HUDSON, NEW YORK

Villa Boscobel stands high above the Hudson River. Boscobel (from the Italian *bosco bello*— beautiful woods) was saved from the wrecker's axe, moved piece by piece from its original site, and rebuilt on the Hudson River opposite historic West Point. It is one of the finest examples of Adam-style architecture in America.

States Morris Dyckman (1755–1806), who built Boscobel for his beloved young wife, Elizabeth, did not live to see his home completed. He was of Dutch descent, worked long in the service of the British Army Quartermaster Corps, and spent part of his life in England. In 1803 he left London to return to his home on the Hudson River with thoughts of building a new house on one of his properties. With his proposed "Mansion house" in mind, he made extensive purchases of glass, silver, china, and a library before leaving England to make his new home as similar to the fine houses he admired in England as he could.

His new home, Boscobel, is unique among Hudson River houses. Its swagged front and two-story portico, side porches, unusual fenestration, with windows much larger than ordinary for the time, and its use of recessed areas and sunken panels on the façade were unprecedented in the locality. In building the house he had the help of a cousin, William Vermilye, a builder in New York; after Dyckman's sudden death in 1806, Vermilye completed the house the following year. It was finished without the intended roofs over the side porches. Dyckman's widow and their son Peter moved into the house in 1807, beginning a century of occupancy by a single family.

In 1920 the estate became a public park, and Boscobel stood empty and neglected. In 1940 demolition was considered, but historical societies and concerned citizens fought to save it. For fifteen years it was under constant threat of demolition. Finally, when the park became a site for a public hospital, the house was declared surplus property and sold to a house wrecker. Old and new champions raised enough money for the purchase of a new site some forty miles north of the original location and for dismantling and erecting anew, restoring and furnishing. From an eminence two hundred feet above the river at Garrison-on-Hudson, the house faces one of the finest prospects in the highlands.

The restoration was completed in 1961. The original woodwork is in place, including the

BEDROOM, VILLA BOSCOBEL

DRAWING ROOM, VILLA BOSCOBEL

semielliptical arches in the hall, and the mantels of the main rooms with their applied Adam ornament. The plasterwork duplicates the original. The interiors are furnished with fine eighteenth- and early nineteenth-century English and American furniture, English silver and ceramics, English and Irish glass, Aubusson and Moorfields carpets.

As one passes from one room to another, one gets the feeling of a home; flowers, fresh and fragrant, quaint toys, the homely charm of vegetables and herbs in the great kitchen, Irish glass gracing the dining room's pedestal table, the lovely toned leather-bound books in the library, the Irish Waterford chandelier in the entrance hall, and the rare Clementi piano in the music room inspire a memory of a time and way of life long ended.

The carriage house reveals farm implements of the period and charming carriages and sleighs

of the preautomobile era. The formal, brick-pathed rose garden shows outstanding landscape architecture. Perhaps it would be most appropriate to close this account of Boscobel in the words of the narration of Helen Hayes, who says in the opening lines of the pageant *Boscobel In Sound And Light,* "Boscobel is the fulfillment of one man's dreams—a fine house beside a broad river. A house to honor a man's ancestors and harbor his progeny."

BOSCOBEL can be reached on highway 9D at Garrison-on-Hudson in New York. It is open April through October from 9:30 A.M. to 5:00 P.M., and November through March from 9:00 A.M. to 4:00 P.M. Boscobel is closed on Tuesday and on New Year's, Thanksgiving, and Christmas days. Admission is $1.50 and children seventy-five cents.

Raynham Hall, like the Townsend family, who lived there for over 150 years, is part of the fabric of Oyster Bay and of the nation. Historically, the most significant period of the eighteenth-century house relates to the founding and establishment of our republic.

In 1738 this house, now known as Raynham Hall, was bought and enlarged by Samuel Townsend, father of Robert ("Culper Jr."), the New York City agent of General George Washington's intelligence service. Samuel Townsend, a merchant, served Oyster Bay for many years as town clerk and justice of the peace. His hearings as king's justice were held in the colonial dining room. After the outbreak of the War for Independence, Samuel Townsend was a member of the New York Provincial Congress that ratified the Declaration of Independence.

Following Long Island's fall to the British, Lieutenant Colonel Simcoe of the Queen's Rangers chose Raynham Hall for his headquarters in the winter of 1778–79. Samuel Townsend's daughters, Audrey, Sally and Phoebe, helped to entertain the British officers and General Sir Henry Clinton's deputy adjutant general, Major John André, a visitor to the Townsend house.

In the Colonial dining room is the famous cupboard where Major André hid freshly fried doughnuts to tease Sally—and later received a fatal message. A conversation between Colonel Simcoe and Major André overheard by Sally in the Colonial hall was relayed to her brother Robert, Culper Jr., secret agent for the American cause. This information led to the disclosure of the Benedict Arnold–André plot to surrender West Point to the British.

About 1851 Solomon Townsend II, grandson of Samuel, added the Victorian Wing and altered the house in the style of the period. Raynham Hall remained in the Townsend family until 1941, when Miss Julia W. Coles gave this historic property to the Oyster Bay Chapter, National Society, Daughters of the American Revolution. In 1947 the organization deeded Raynham Hall to the Town of Oyster Bay, while maintaining and continuing its active concern for the building. Since that time the Town of Oyster Bay has restored the building and grounds.

To walk through the Colonial rooms where such stirring events occurred and through the Victorian Wing, which mirrors the taste and life of the mid-nineteenth century, is an exciting tour. In the Colonial Garden are two large iron links from the great chain that spanned the Hudson River at West Point in 1778 as a barrier to the British Fleet.

RAYNHAM HALL is almost seven miles north of Exit 35 of Northern State Parkway in Long Island's Nassau County. It is west of Sagamore Hill. It is located on West Main Street in the town of Oyster Bay. It is open to the public daily except Tuesdays from 10:00 A.M. to 12:00 noon and from 1:00 P.M. to 5:00 P.M. Adults are admitted for fifty cents; children accompanied by adults are admitted free.

VANDERBILT MANSION

HYDE PARK, NEW YORK

Vanderbilt Mansion is an impressive example of the great estates developed by financial and industrial leaders in the era following the Civil War. It was the country home of Frederick W. Vanderbilt, a grandson of "Commodore" Cornelius Vanderbilt, who founded the family fortune in steamboating and railroading. The mansion was designed and built in 1896–98 by the famous architectural firm of McKim, Mead, and White. It is one of the finest examples of Italian Renaissance architecture in the United States.

The history of the 211-acre grounds goes back much further than that of the mansion. The grounds had been maintained as a country seat by prominent individuals since colonial days. The fine old trees and spreading lawns had been carefully developed for generations. Hyde Park, as the estate was first called, is said to have been named by Peter Fauconnier, the private secretary of Edward Hyde, Viscount Cornbury, later third Earl of Clarendon and governor of New York from 1702 to 1708. Fauconnier held office in the colony as collector and receiver general and also owned extensive tracts of land, including a part of the patent of Hyde Park. This patent was granted in the reign of Queen Anne on April 18, 1705. The town of Hyde Park was established in 1821 and took its name from the estate.

Following the death of Fauconnier in 1746, Hyde Park had a succession of owners. One, Dr. David Hosack, was deeply interested in plants, trees, and flowers. He engaged André Parmentier, a Belgian landscape gardener, to lay out roads, walks, and scenic vistas. This work was probably done between 1828 and 1830. The rare and exotic specimens that grace the lawns and park appear to date, for the most part, from that time. In 1840, five years after the death of Dr. Hosack, John Jacob Astor bought the mansion tract and made a gift of the estate to his daughter, Dorothea Astor Langdon, and her children. In 1895 Hyde Park was offered for sale again and was purchased by Frederick W. Vanderbilt. Mr. Vanderbilt had the Langdon House torn down and on its site he erected the present Vanderbilt Mansion. It was completed in 1898 at a cost of $660,000 without furnishings. Care was used in choosing the furnishings; continental motifs, especially Italian and French, predominate. The grounds were improved, and new farm buildings, carriage houses, and entranceways were built. Mr. Vanderbilt's niece, Mrs. Margaret Van Alen, donated the estate to the United States to be used as a national historic site.

The reception room on the first floor has Italian marble. The mantel is from an Italian palace, and the old throne chairs around the walls are also of Italian origin. Two French Renaissance cabinets stand at either side of the doorway. The woodwork in the study is Santo Domingo mahogany. A hand-carved Renaissance panel forms the back of the desk chair. Italian pistols are grouped above an old Flemish clock above the fireplace. The library is decorated with wood carvings by a Swiss artist. The guns on the wall are antique wheel locks. There are sixteenth-century Brussels tapestries in the south foyer. The furniture of the drawing room is pre-dominantly French. Florentine tapestries on the end walls bear the coat of arms of the Medici family. The twin fireplaces are of Italian marble. The gold room is a French salon modeled after an eighteenth-century French drawing room. The standing clock is a copy of one in the Louvre. The north foyer has a Florentine storage chest of hand-carved wood with gold leaf and lacquer. The thirty-by-fifty-foot dining room has a huge Ispahan rug. The dining room furniture is a reproduction of Louis XIV. At either side of the doorway are eighteenth-century planetaria. There are two Renaissance mantels and an old Italian ceiling. The stairway lead-

MRS. F. W. VANDERBILT'S BEDROOM

DRAWING ROOM, VANDERBILT HOME

ing to the second floor is old Italian marble. Italian busts and statues occupy the niches along the way.

The second floor's north foyer has a Louis XVI table. The chandelier is of beaded crystal. The blue room is the largest of the guest rooms. It has a white onyx French clock and a rare old prayer rug (Ghiordes). The mauve room is a guest room with a finely woven Persian dowry rug in the center. The pieces on the mantel are of the French Empire period. Mr. Vanderbilt's room has carved woodwork of Circassian walnut from Russia and walls covered with seventeenth-century Flemish tapestry. Mrs. Vanderbilt's room is a reproduction of a French queen's bedroom of the Louis XV period. The wall at the head of the bed is covered with hand-embroidered silk. The other walls are wood paneled inset with French paintings. The furniture is a reproduction by Sormani of French Louis XV period pieces.

The third floor contains five additional guest rooms and rooms for seventeen maids. It is not open to visitors.

VANDERBILT MANSION is on the New York–Albany Post Road, U.S. 9, at the northern edge of Hyde Park, New York, about six miles north of Poughkeepsie, New York. The mansion is closed on Monday except from June 15 through Labor Day. It is open from 9:00 A.M. to 5:00 P.M. There is a "nominal" admission charge. Children under twelve are admitted free.

DINING ROOM, VANDERBILT HOME

The William Trent House on South Warren Street is the oldest mansion in the community and one of the outstanding examples of Queen Anne architecture in America. William Trent, later New Jersey's first chief justice, from whom the city of Trenton derives its name, built it in 1719.

William Trent emigrated from his native Inverness, Scotland, with his brother James about 1682. They settled in Philadelphia, where he identified himself in business with the Quakers. He soon became a large wholesale and re-

tail merchant and a shipowner in partnership with William Penn and James Logan. From 1703 to 1710 Trent was a member of the Pennsylvania Provincial Council and was selected to systematize the courts. Later he was one of the five Supreme Court justices. In 1710, 1715, and 1719 he was a member of the Assembly, and in 1717–18 was Speaker of the House. In Philadelphia, as in Trenton, William Trent was a large landowner. His residence in that city was the famous "Slate Roof House" on Second Street, which had been William Penn's mansion—the most elegant in the city.

In 1714 Trent purchased from Mahlon Stacy the younger eight hundred acres of land lying on both sides of Assunpink Creek at the Falls of the Delaware; afterwards he bought additional lands from others. On these broad acres he built the brick mansion where it is thought he spent two summers until his final settlement there in 1721. At that time he had a township laid out, which he called Trent Town.

From Governor Burnet of New Jersey he received a commission as colonel of the Hunterdon County Militia. He represented Burlington County in the Assembly in 1722, becoming speaker in 1723. The Governor made Trent judge of the Court of Common Pleas in Hunterdon County in 1719 and in 1723 appointed him Chief Justice of New Jersey. He died suddenly on Christmas Day, 1724.

In 1729, several years after Justice Trent's death his eldest son, James, conveyed the property by deed to William Morris, a wealthy merchant from the West Indies. From that time on it changed hands many times. Lewis Morris, a colonial governor, leased the house for four years. In fact, the mansion has been three times a residence of governors and knew days of gaiety and wide hospitality just after the Revolution, when Colonel and Mrs. John Cox and their six daughters kept continual open house. It was then known as "Bloomsbury Court." A contemporary account described the house as "a genteel brick dwelling, 40 x 48 feet, two stories high, four rooms on a floor, with a large handsome staircase and entry, with a cellar under the whole building, and a court yard on each front of the house, one fronting down the River Delaware through a large handsome avenue of English cherry trees to the ferry the other fronting up the river to Trenton." The house as restored today is more than eighty percent original, and the "large handsome staircase and entry" referred to are completely untouched. The restoration was started in 1934, and the house was formally dedicated on October 14, 1936.

Furnishings of the period of William and

156

Mary and of Queen Anne have been assembled to approximate those of an inventory made in 1726 to settle Trent's estate. A number of the pieces chosen for the house are of English origin, inasmuch as it was assumed that Trent, as a man of wealth with his own ships in the London trade, often ordered furniture from abroad. The garden is planted along the lines suggested by references to the Trent garden.

The WILLIAM TRENT HOUSE is located on South Warren Street in Trenton, New Jersey. From May through August it is open on weekdays from 10:00 A.M. to 5:00 P.M. and on Sunday from 1:00 P.M. to 4:00 P.M. From September through April it is open on weekdays from 10:00 A.M. to 4:00 P.M. and on Sunday from 1:00 P.M. to 4:00 P.M. Admission is twenty-five cents, children ten cents.

WILLIAM TRENT HOUSE

THE DAVID WILSON MANSION

ODESSA, DELAWARE

David Wilson (1743–1820) was a prosperous merchant and member of the Society of Friends. His store stood just east of his house on Main Street, directly in front of the present Corbit-Sharp House, built in 1772 by William Corbit. His first wife was Margaret Empson; his second wife, Mary Corbit, was the sister of William Corbit. At David Wilson's death his property passed to his children, David and Rachel, the son retaining the house and store. The son first married Ann Jefferis, the daughter of the sea captain who owned the ship *Brothers*. The Wilsons lived in the Mansion until 1830, when, against the advice of his friends, David Jr. sold everything and moved to Indiana.

His house, store, and surrounding land were bought by William Polk, a resident of Cantwell's Bridge, as Odessa was then called. The new owner made various changes, including the addition of the third story on the rear wing. The house was owned by William Polk and his descendants until 1901, when his granddaughter sold it to Mary Corbit Warner, a granddaughter of David Wilson, Jr. At Mrs. Warner's death in 1923 the mansion, under her will, became a museum to display her collections and to house the Corbit Library.

The main section of the house, of Colonial Georgian style, was built by David Wilson in 1769. The entrance doorway's Doric columns and pitch pediment reveal the eighteenth-century interest in classical architecture. Above the finely proportioned windows are cut stone lintels, and the roof cornice is set off by a distinctive row of applied dentils. Directly behind the kitchen fireplace is the smoke house. This small structure not only covered the projecting baking ovens but also made use of the cooking smoke

to preserve meats hung from the rafters. Beyond the smoke house are the usual dependencies necessary to the eighteenth-century way of life. The back wing of the house, however, is of an earlier date (c. 1747), and when it was restored in 1962, many interesting details were discovered. A fireplace in the dining room is faced with King of Prussia marble and contains a cast-iron fire-back. The kitchen has a winding stairway at one side of the fireplace and the unusual feature of two Dutch ovens.

The interior is distinguished by fine paneled room-ends. The fireplace in the drawing room is flanked by butterfly cupboards. Similar paneling is seen in the two well-proportioned principal second floor bedrooms. Although the house contains some original pieces of family furniture as well as many of the Corbit and Wilson papers, books, and memorabilia, much of the present handsome eighteenth-century furniture was donated in 1943.

The Corbit Library was founded in 1847 under the will of Dr. James Corbit, a grandson of William Corbit, who died in 1846 and bequeathed his private library. This library, the first free library in Delaware, was moved to the David Wilson Mansion in 1924, where, it is still maintained.

The DAVID WILSON MANSION is located in Odessa, 23 miles south of Wilmington, Delaware, and 23 miles north of Dover, Delaware, on Route 13, the DuPont Parkway. It is open on Tuesday, Thursday, and Saturday from 10:00 A.M. to 5:00 P.M. and on Sunday from 2:00 P.M. to 5:00 P.M. from April 1 to December 1. Admission is fifty cents, children twenty-five cents.

THE CARTER HOUSE

FRANKLIN, TENNESSEE

Carter House, caught in the swirling center of one of the bloodiest battles of the War Between the States, was designed and built in 1830 by its first owner, Fountain Branch Carter, with the aid of Negro slaves who cut the timber and made the sun-dried brick. Three generations of the Carter family lived in this lovely house distinguished by its pleasing proportions, its stone-capped end gables, its graceful double front door flanked by free Doric columns, its fanlight of hand-poured glass, and its two large front windows that repeat the door design.

About one o'clock in the morning on November 30, 1864, federal troops under General Jacob D. Cox awakened the Carter family and commandeered the house as the Federal Command Post. General Cox's mission was to hold the advancing forces of Confederate General Hood in order to allow the army of General John Schofield to join with the Federal forces of General George H. Thomas, which were at Nashville, eighteen miles north of Franklin. General Cox took command of both divisions of the Twenty-Third Corps. The Federals' main line of defense was only 204 feet south of the Carter House, and breastworks were erected and topped with logs torn from the Carter barns. The inner Federal entrenchment was only sixty feet south of the Carter House and was in line with the smoke house and office. All communications came to the Carter House until the battle was over.

It was daylight on November 30 when General Hood learned that Schofield's army had evaded him. He marched toward Franklin in pursuit. When he arrived at Winstead Hill, two miles south of Franklin and commanding a view of the entire valley, he could see Cox's forces entrenched on the southern outskirts of the town near the Carter House. Against the advice of his generals, Hood ordered a frontal attack. In wave upon wave the twenty thousand Confederates came in splendid array, bands playing and flags flying. Repeated heroic assaults were met with equally determined defense. For five hours the dreadful fighting continued; at midnight the fighting stopped. With the coming of dawn General Hood discovered that the Federal army had withdrawn during the night and was already moving toward Nashville to join the forces of General Thomas. General Hood paid dearly for his assault; 6,252 men were killed, missing, or wounded and twelve Confederate generals were casualties—five dead. The Battle of Franklin marked the beginning of the end in the estimation of General Cox.

One of the tragic, yet dramatic, incidents of the Battle of Franklin was the death of Captain Theodrick Carter, who fought with General Hood's army. He was found mortally wounded only 175 yards from his own home. His aged father and sister found him and carried him into his home where he died forty-eight hours later. The Rev. Henry M. Field wrote, "It is something which is not always given a soldier to draw his last breath under his father's roof, and to be laid in his last sleep beside the dust of his kindred."

Today the basement museum holds interesting documents, uniforms, flags, guns, and maps of the battlefield.

The CARTER HOUSE is located in Franklin, Tennessee, on U. S. Highway 31. It is open Monday through Saturday from 9:00 A.M. to 4:30 P.M. and on Sunday from 2:00 P.M. to 4:30 P.M..

VICKSBURG, MISSISSIPPI

Candon Hearth is the only ante bellum home that was situated on the actual defense lines of the Confederate forces during the seige of Vicksburg in 1863. It was built in the early 1840s. It stands on one of the highest knolls in Vicksburg and can be seen from many distant points in the city. During the Yankee bombardment on June 4, 1863, a cannon ball pierced the walls of the house and beheaded William Newman, the original settler. Candon Hearth was literally peppered with shells and minie balls during the long siege of Vicksburg. Some of the holes may still be seen, including that made by the ball that killed Mr. Newman. He was

buried under a tree still standing in the front yard. Later his body was reinterred in the Vicksburg City Cemetery. Also to be seen is the only original slave chest known to be shown in the South. It is riddled by minie balls.

Candon Hearth has been preserved rather than restored. Its oversized, hand-hewn timbers and cottage-type farmhouse design reminiscent of revolutionary and prerevolutionary architecture are familiar and distinctive. Most of the original structure of cypress, pine, and other materials is intact. The original twelve-inch-wide plank flooring still remains as subflooring under the modern hardwood. The original four-paneled doors with porcelain knobs are still there.

Throughout the house there are interesting antique features: the chimney and fireplace made of original bricks from ante bellum days; an oversized octagonal glass salt-cellar; first editions; Civil War relics and articles found hidden in loft timbers and battlefield yard. Some of the siege trenches are still to be found on the estate.

CANDON HEARTH is located at 2530 South Confederate Avenue in the Vicksburg National Military Park. It is open daily from dawn to dusk. Admission is $1.00, children twenty-five cents.

CANDON HEARTH

FREMONT, NORTH CAROLINA

North Carolina's "Educational Governor," Charles Brantley Aycock, was born November 1, 1859, in a very plain farmhouse in Wayne County near Fremont. From this humble beginning he went on to be elected governor of North Carolina in 1901.

To a great extent Aycock used his administration to strengthen and better the public school system of the state. His educational program for increased school taxes, consolidation of one-room schools, building of additional schoolhouses, longer school terms, and higher salaries for teachers earned him the title of "Educational Governor."

Aycock's 1912 campaign for the United States Senate was cut short by his sudden death in Birmingham, Alabama, on April 4, while he was delivering his famous speech on universal education. Today his life and work remain an inspiration to North Carolinians interested in public education.

The Charles B. Aycock Birthplace not only shows the house in which Aycock was born but also a typical eastern North Carolina farmhouse and outbuildings of the mid-1800s. The site includes a dwelling house, four farm buildings, a restored 1870 one-room school and a Visitors' Center–Museum.

The school was built in 1870 and has been restored and furnished in the style of that period. It serves a twofold purpose; as an educational exhibit it is typical of rural schools in existence at the time Aycock became Governor; and as an assembly room it is used for lectures to visitor groups.

The Visitor Center–Museum houses the exhibits that portray Aycock's adult life (with special emphasis on his educational progress) the administrative office, and research area.

The CHARLES B. AYCOCK BIRTHPLACE is located in North Carolina one-half mile east of U.S. 117 between Pikeville and Fremont and twelve miles north of Goldsboro. It is open Monday to Friday from 8:00 A.M. to 5:00 P.M. and on Sundays from 1:00 P.M. to 5:00 P.M. It is closed on Saturdays, Thanksgiving, and Christmas. Admission is twenty-five cents, children ten cents.

WILLIAMSBURG, VIRGINIA

Two hundred and ten years ago Carter's Grove was the home of the influential Burwell family and was one of the plantations that anchored the world of the Virginia planter aristocracy. Located on the James River, it was a meeting place for influential Virginians. Its gay social events also attracted the leading men of the day. Carter Burwell, the builder, was a member of the House of Burgesses. His son, Nathaniel, was a member of the Constitutional Convention of 1778.

The handsome Georgian house was built between 1750 and 1753. A team composed of David Minetree and John Wheatley, both of Williamsburg, built the basic framework of the house. A woodworker, Richard Bayliss, was im-ported from England to do the interior wood-work.

Five generations of Burwells lived in Carter's Grove before it was sold out of the family in 1838. During the next hundred years the planta-tion had a series of owners and tenants. The late Mr. and Mrs. Archibald M. McCrea, the most recent private owners, purchased it in 1927. Their restoration consisted of enlarging and joining the two flanking buildings (the office and kitchen) to the central house and add-ing a third floor with dormers. A modern porch was also removed, and paint was stripped from the paneled interiors.

The present house of five connected parts is two hundred feet long, looking over green ter-

CARTER'S GROVE PLANTATION

races to the James River. The brick walls of the main house are in Flemish bond above the ground-floor level and in English bond below. The kitchen and office are also in Flemish bond but have the patterned glazed headers characteristic of early eighteenth-century brick masonry. The kitchen was built about 1700, the office several years later.

The entrance hall and stair hall are noted for their unusual paneling and carved woodwork. It is considered "the finest room in all Georgian architecture." Other first floor rooms include the library, dining room, parlor or "Refusal Room," drawing room, the kitchen and office wings, and the two connecting rooms between the wings and the main house. In the "Refusal Room," famous for its mantel of white and Sienna marble and its carvel frieze panel, both Washington and Jefferson, according to tradition, were refused marriage by two Virginia belles. Mary Cary turned down Washington; Rebecca Burwell refused Jefferson.

There are eight bedrooms on the second floor including the wings, and three on the third. The furnishings include seventeenth- and eighteenth-century antiques as well as later pieces.

CARTER'S GROVE is six miles east of Williamsburg on U. S. Route 60. It is open from 10:00 A.M. to 5:00 P.M. daily from mid-March to the Sunday following Thanksgiving. Admission is $1.50, preschool children, free.

GREAT ENTRANCE HALL, CARTER'S GROVE PLANTATION

COLONIAL WILLIAMSBURG

WILLIAMSBURG, VIRGINIA

From 1699 to 1780 Williamsburg was the capital of the Virginia Colony and the focus of a proud plantation society. It was the ideological training ground for leaders of the American independence movement and a social, cultural, and political center ranking in importance with Boston, Philadelphia, and New York. There George Washington, Patrick Henry, George Wythe, Thomas Jefferson, George Mason, Edmund Pendleton, and other leaders laid the foundations of our government. There Patrick Henry delivered his famous speech in support of his Resolution Against the Stamp Act. The "May 15th, 1776 Resolution for Independence," which influenced the historic Fourth of July Declaration of Independence, was adopted there. After 1780, when the capital was moved to Richmond, Williamsburg stepped backstage in history and resumed its role only when restoration was begun in 1926.

In 1926 John D. Rockefeller Jr. became interested in the restoration of eighteenth-century Williamsburg. His purpose and that of the trustees was "to re-create accurately the environment of the men and women of eighteenth-century Williamsburg and to bring about such an understanding of their lives and times that present and future generations may more vividly appreciate the contribution of these early Americans to the ideals and culture of our country."

The Historic Area of Williamsburg covers 130 acres and is located in the heart of the city of Williamsburg. It is a mile long, with the Wren Building of the College of William and Mary at the western extremity and the capitol at the eastern end. Its average width is one-half mile, and it embraces the buildings fronting on the three principal longitudinal streets of the city—Duke of Gloucester, Francis, and Nicholson Streets. Within this area stand eighty-five of Williamsburg's eighteenth-century houses, shops, taverns, public and other buildings that have survived to the present time. They have been saved, stripped of nineteenth- and twentieth-century additions, and restored to their original condition. Among them are the Wren Building, the President's House, and the Brafferton at the College; the Courthouse of 1770; Bruton Parish Church; the Public Magazine; Market Square Tavern; and many fine residences, including the George Wythe, Peyton Randolph, Brush-Everard, and St. George Tucker houses.

To complete the scene an additional fifty major buildings and a large number of smaller structures have been rebuilt on original sites after extensive archaeological, architectural, and historical research. The Governor's Palace and

THE CAPITOL, WILLIAMSBURG

the Capitol are prime examples, and they play an essential part in the interpretation of many of the historic events that took place there in the eighteenth century. More than eighty acres of gardens and greens have been made to live again in their eighteenth-century forms. The Historic Area also includes a small number of original nineteenth-century buildings, but no structures of any type are moved into the Area to give any additional, unauthentic colonial atmosphere. More than 3,000 acres surrounding the Historic Area have been purchased as a protective measure.

There are seven principal exhibition properties: the Governor's Palace, the Capitol, Raleigh Tavern, Public Magazine, Gaol, George Wythe House, and Brush-Everard House. These seven properties encompass more than forty buildings with approximately 150 rooms furnished primarily with American and English antiques. In addition to the seven major properties there are twelve craft shops where costumed craftsmen employ hand methods and the tools of the eighteenth century to fashion articles similar to those made by their colonial predecessors. These shops include the apothecary, baker, blacksmith and gunsmith, bootmaker, cabinetmaker, candlemaker, miller, milliner, printer and bookbinder, silversmith and clockmaker, spinner and weaver, and wigmaker. In the summer months such crafts as flax-breaking, pewter-casting, papermaking, shinglemaking and soapmaking are practiced outdoors.

THE HALL OF THE VIRGINIA HOUSE OF BURGESSES, WILLIAMSBURG

169

COLONIAL WILLIAMSBURG *is situated on a peninsula between the James and York Rivers. It can be reached by taking U.S. Route 60 from Richmond or State Route 132 or 168 from Richmond. Inside Colonial Williamsburg there is constant free bus service between areas and buildings. One can board and leave buses at will. Costumed hostesses impart the history of these buildings and interesting facts about the colonial inhabitants during frequent tours, which originate at each major building. A combination ticket purchased at the Information Center will admit you to each major building. The combination ticket costs $3.00 for adults and $1.00 for children 7 to 11 years of age. Colonial Williamsburg is open year round.*

GEORGE WYTHE HOUSE, WILLIAMSBURG

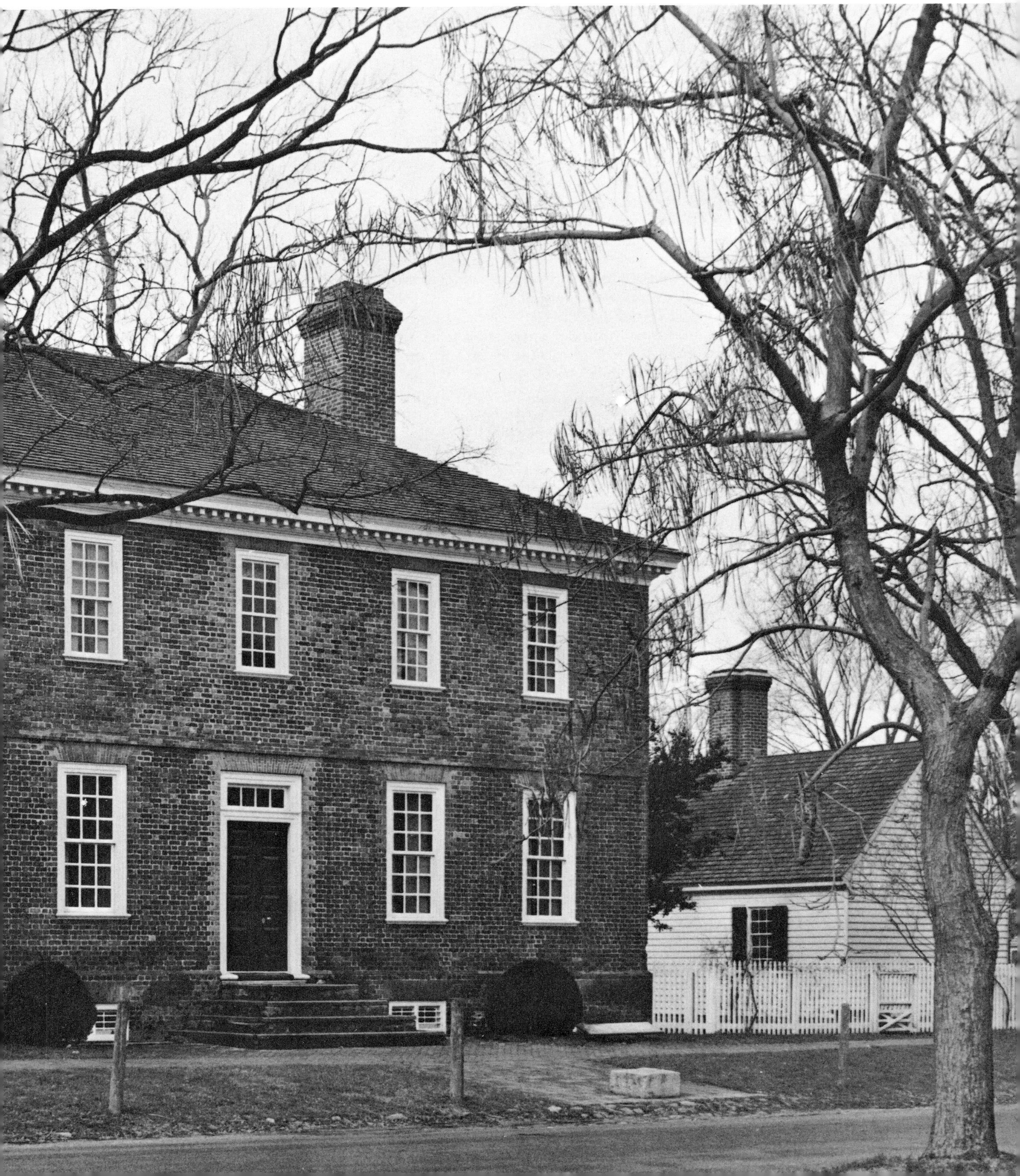

CRAGMORE

GALLATIN, TENNESSEE

Cragmore was the home of revolutionary hero General James Winchester, a founder of Memphis. Together with Andrew Jackson and John Overton he probably gave the name Cragmore to this house built on a rocky bluff surrounded by streams. The house resembles those of the late Georgian period in New England. The General brought stone masons and ship carpenters seven hundred miles through the wilderness from his native state, Maryland, to build the house. The stone was quarried on the place and the fine workmanship of the masons can be seen in the fitted limestone blocks braced with long iron rods running the length of the house to brace and balance the construction.

The poplar, walnut, cherry, and ash used in the frame were hand hewn and cut out of the virgin forest. In the attic the beams were put together with wooden pegs. The nails were hand wrought. The stenciled walls in the parlor give evidence of traveling artists 160 years ago. The ballroom on the second floor has galleries on either side from which one sees lovely views of the garden and rolling farm land. Lafayette was entertained there on his visit in 1824. Andrew Jackson, Sam Houston, and John Overton often enjoyed the hospitality of Cragmore.

In the basement can be seen the typical weaving room and wine cellar, both important during frontier days. One of the interesting sights in the house is the completely restored kitchen. Hams, bread, cakes, pies, and biscuits are sold from this kitchen hearth to visitors.

General Winchester died in 1826 and is buried in the family plot near the flower garden.

CRAGMORE is located five miles east of Gallatin on Highway 25 in Sumner County. It is open every weekday except Monday from 10:00 A.M. to 5:00 P.M. and on Sunday from 1:00 P.M. to 6:00 P.M. It is open from April 15 until October 15. Admission is fifty cents, children twenty-five cents.

ARLINGTON, VIRGINIA

The Custis-Lee Mansion is distinctive primarily because of its long association with the families of Custis, Washington, and Lee. It is now a memorial to Robert E. Lee. It was the home of George Washington Parke Custis, the foster son of the first President, and for years was the treasury of both the Washington heirlooms and the Washington tradition. Robert E. Lee, a young lieutenant in the U. S. Army, and Mary Custis, great-granddaughter of Martha Washington, married and reared a family there. And there Colonel Robert E. Lee made his decision to serve the South. Today Arlington House, as it was formerly known, furnished with appointments of its early period, preserves the atmosphere of gracious living typical of that romantic age of American history.

George Washington Parke Custis, builder of Arlington House, was the grandson of Martha Washington and the foster son of George Washington. Martha Custis was a widow with two children when she married George Washington. When her son John Parke Custis died at the close of the Revolutionary War, he left four

CUSTIS-LEE MANSION

children. George Washington adopted the two youngest. They were reared at Mount Vernon. In 1802, the year Martha Washington died, her grandson began building Arlington House on the 1,100-acre estate his father had purchased from the Alexander family in 1778. The house was to receive the legacy of his grandmother— furniture and pictures, plate and china from Mount Vernon, and, more precious still, personal effects of George Washington. Two years later, at the age of twenty-three, he was married to Mary Lee Fitzhugh of Alexandria and Chatham.

Plans for the building were drawn by George Hadfield, a young English architect. The north wing was built first, and the south wing was completed in 1804. The foundation stone and the timber came from the estate. The bricks were made from native clay. The portico and large center section were not finished until 1817.

One of the pleasant incidents in the history of the house was the visit in 1824 of General Lafayette, who pronounced the view from the portico unrivaled and entreated Mrs. Custis never to sacrifice any of the fine trees.

On June 30, 1831, Mary Ann Randolph Custis, only child of the Arlington Custis family,

became the wife of Lt. Robert E. Lee, a young West Point graduate. The wedding ceremony took place in the family parlor of the mansion. Much of Mrs. Lee's married life was spent at the mansion. Six of the seven Lee children were born there. The Arlington plantation was sadly run down, and Robert E. Lee felt that his presence at Arlington was necessary if he was to give proper attention to the estate. He obtained extended leave and settled down to the life of a farmer. More than two years elapsed before he rejoined his regiment. During that period the traditions of Arlington House were maintained, and it was a favorite stopping place for relatives and friends.

Following the news of the secession of Virginia, Lee, than a colonel, resigned his commission in the U. S. Army and, at the request of the governor of Virginia, departed for Richmond. Mrs. Lee remained at Arlington, dismantling her home and sending her family possessions to a place of safety. Soon after she left, Federal troops occupied the lands between Washington and Alexandria. Situated on the line of fortifications guarding Washington, the Arlington estate became an armed camp. Headquarters were established in the mansion. When Mrs.

STATE DINING ROOM, CUSTIS-LEE MANSION

Lee was unable to appear personally to pay taxes, as was required, the government confiscated the property; about two hundred acres were set aside for a national cemetery in June, 1864. Upon the death of Mrs. Lee in 1873, Custis Lee took steps to recover the Arlington property. The U. S. Supreme Court gave him a favorable decision, and he sold the property to the United States for $150,000.

The Custis-Lee Mansion's front with its two wings extends 140 feet. The wings are identical except that in the north wing the space corresponding to the state dining room in the south wing was divided into small rooms for the temporary accomodation of Mr. and Mrs. Custis while the house was being built. It was never changed. The central portion is divided by a wide central hall. A large formal drawing room with two fine marble fireplaces lies south of this hall. To the north of it one can see the family dining room and family parlor separated by a north and south partition which is broken by three graceful arches. The second story is also divided by a central hall on either side of which there are two bedrooms and accompanying dressing rooms. A small room used as a linen closet is at the end of this hall. The third floor

was used only for storage purposes and remained an unfinished attic. The grand portico facing the Potomac has eight massive Doric columns and is sixty feet wide and twenty-five feet deep. At the rear two buildings form a courtyard. They were used as servants' quarters, smokehouse, workroom, and summer kitchen.

For years after the war, the mansion was an empty shell used only as an office for the superintendent of the cemetery. In 1925, the Secretary of War was empowered to restore Arlington House to its ante bellum condition. Furniture known to have been in the mansion and replicas of pieces of that furniture were procured. Other pieces suitable to the first half of the nineteenth century were also obtained. Today the Custis-Lee Mansion appears almost exactly as it did back in that century.

The CUSTIS-LEE MANSION is located in Arlington National Cemetery. You can get there from Washington, D.C., by bus or car via the Arlington Memorial Bridge to the mansion. It is open from 9:30 A.M. to 4:30 P.M. from October through March, and from 9:30 A.M. to 6:00 P.M. from April through September. There is a small admission charge, which is waived for children.

KITCHEN, CUSTIS-LEE MANSION

DAVENPORT HOUSE

SAVANNAH, GEORGIA

This unusual and beautiful example of late Georgian architecture was built in 1815 by master builder Isaiah Davenport for his own use. It ranks among the great Georgian houses of America. Its severe simplicity is enhanced by delicate ironwork and an elliptical stairway. Elements of Regency and Greek revival combined with Georgian design make Davenport House especially interesting to architectural connoisseurs. The drawing room, with its eighteen-branch crystal chandelier, is considered one of the most beautiful rooms in Savannah. (Measured drawings of the house are now kept in the Library of Congress.)

The fine furnishings, which reflect the grace and elegance of the Georgian period, come mostly from the Savannah area. Among them are heirlooms of the Davenport family. Since the builder was closely related to John Davenport, a famous eighteenth-century potter, the house features a fine collection of ancestral Davenport china as well as Spode, Chinese Export, and Philadelphia Tucker china pieces.

As the City of Savannah moved outward, Davenport House, along with other fine old downtown homes, found itself becoming a slum in a neglected neighborhood. It was saved from destruction by the Historic Savannah Foundation and is now partially restored and serves as the Foundation's headquarters.

DAVENPORT HOUSE is located on East State Street facing Columbia Square. It is open to the public Monday through Saturday from 10:30 A.M. to 1:00 P.M. and from 2:30 P.M. to 5:00 P.M. It is closed on Sundays and national holidays. Admission is seventy-five cents, children twenty-five cents.

DRAWING ROOM, DAVENPORT HOUSE

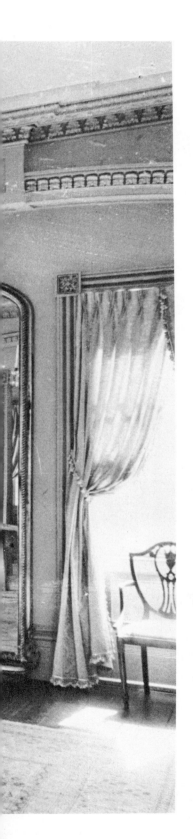

THE DECATUR HOUSE

WASHINGTON, D. C.

In 1816 the thirty-seven-year-old Naval hero Commodore Stephen Decatur came to Washington to serve on the Board of Navy Commissioners. Prize money won by his daring exploits enabled him to buy Washington real estate, including nineteen lots on the President's Square. For the site of his town house he chose a small plot of land opposite the northwest corner of the Square; he then selected as the designer of his house Benjamin Henry Latrobe, America's first professional architect.

In January, 1819, Commodore Decatur and his wife, Susan Wheeler, moved into their new home, designed in the restrained elegance of the Federal period; during their fourteen-month occupancy they made it the social center of Washington. On March 22, Decatur fought his fatal duel with Commodore James Barron and was brought home a dying man. The grief-stricken widow left the house and never returned. It was sold many years later.

Political, social and diplomatic intrigue flourished in the house under a succession of distinguished tenants. First it became the French legation and then the Russian legation; later it was the residence of the British minister. Three secretaries of state lived in Decatur House—Henry Clay, Martin Van Buren, and Edward Livingston. In 1877 it was purchased by Mary Edwards Beale, wife of General Edward Fitzgerald Beale. The Beale family owned and occupied the house until 1956, when Mrs. Truxtun Beale bequeathed Decatur House to the National Trust. In 1944 Mrs. Beale retained the late Thomas Tileston Waterman as architect for the restoration, which was based on eleven original Latrobe drawings. Decatur House is the only original house on President's Square to survive the changes of almost 150 years.

Decatur House is furnished with many valuable pieces of antique furniture, glass, art, statuary, and military mementos. The first-floor hall contains a pair of nineteenth-century Italian walnut desks, two blue-and-white Nanking China cylindrical vases, and paintings of two Arabian stallions that were presented to U. S. Grant by the Sultan of Turkey. The first floor library has documents signed by James Monroe and U. S. Grant, a portrait and bust of Edward F. Beale, and a ceremonial dagger and sword case. The first floor garden room has additional documents signed by Benjamin H. Harrison and James G. Blaine and a number of oil paintings of western scenes. The first-floor dining room has Fitzhugh China in a Sheraton-style cabinet, ten pieces of inscribed silver, and the Truxtun Urn, presented at Lloyds Coffee House in London to Captain Thomas Truxtun of the American Frigate *Constellation* for his service in taking the French Frigate *Insurgente* in the West Indies in 1799.

The parquetry flooring of California woods in the second floor drawing room was put in for the Beales. There are also six nineteenth-century Kakemona Japanese drawings, an eighteenth-century red lacquer Portuguese table, a Belter chair, and elaborate ceiling decorations painted during the Civil War. The second floor garden room contains books from the library of Edward F. Beale that were carried to sea on the Frigate *Congress*. The flooring is the original one.

DECATUR HOUSE is located on Lafayette Square at 748 Jackson Place, N. W. in Washington, D.C. It is open daily from 10:00 A.M. to 4:00 P.M. It is closed on Christmas Day. Admission is fifty cents.

FARMINGTON

LEXINGTON, KENTUCKY

This beautiful fourteen-room federal-style house was built by John Speed on a tract of land granted to his father, James Speed, a captain in the Revolutionary War. James Speed received the land in 1780 from Patrick Henry, then Governor of Virginia. (In 1780 Kentucky was a Virginia county.) The original deed is on display at Farmington.

In 1808 John Speed married Lucy Fry and

began to build on the 1,000-acre site. As his bride's happiest memories were of her uncle's home in Charlottesville, Virginia, which was designed by Thomas Jefferson and also named *Farmington,* John Speed arranged for their Jefferson-designed home to bear the same name.

Farmington was by choice and necessity a large, self-sufficient establishment. Indian troubles had eased, but the country people were still wary of both white and Indian marauders. Five hundred acres were under cultivation. Food was produced, livestock was raised, flax was grown and woven into cloth, candles and

soap were made, and almost all clothing was made at home. Hemp was the biggest crop (eighty-seven acres), and much of it was made into rope. Seventy slaves were needed to carry on such extensive activity. After John Speed's death and before the Emancipation Proclamation, Mrs. Speed freed the slaves.

One of the Speed sons, Joshua, went to Springfield, Illinois, after college. There he became a storekeeper and formed a lifelong friendship with Abraham Lincoln. When his father died, Joshua returned to Farmington to help his mother manage the estate. Lincoln came to Farmington for a three-week visit when he was despondent over a quarrel with his bride-to-be, Mary Todd. He played a role in Joshua's romance with Fanny Henning that led to their marriage. The next year, Lincoln married Mary Todd.

Farmington was designed by Thomas Jefferson, and the master builder, Edward Shippen, who directed the construction and made only minor modifications in the design. Farmington graphically illustrates Jeffersonian characteristics—the most notable being the two octagonal rooms. Other Jeffersonian features include the classic portico with Doric columns and exterior fanlight, the balanced, orderly plan of the rooms, the enclosed stairways (Jefferson believed open stairways wasted space and heat), the hinged window panels, interior fanlights, and the one-story-above-a-basement plan, which gives air and light to the basement.

The house contains fourteen rooms. The upstairs ceilings are fourteen feet high. The basement has an interior room that originally had a dirt floor and may have served as a wine cellar. There were many other outbuildings. Among them were the smokehouse, henhouse, stables, schoolhouse, slave cabins, and blacksmith shop. The remains of a stone building, the spring house, and the ice house still exist. The two-story log house was discovered on River Road, dismantled and reconstructed here. The kitchen garden is typical of the old days, with its combination of vegetables, fruits, herbs, and flowers. The flower borders were always an integral part of the kitchen garden. There was always a profusion of bulbs, peonies, iris, sweet william, lemon lilies, clove pinks and many other flowers.

The period to which the house is restored is 1810–20, the first ten years after it was built. There are no original furnishings other than Elizabeth's Speed's china tea set and the little pewter tea set that belonged to the Speed children. Curtains and upholstery throughout the house, though new, are authentic designs of the period. All the rugs are old orientals. The one in the front hall is Anatolian; the ones in the study, sitting room, and blue bedroom are Kermanshah; the parlor has a Mahal and the dining room a Sheruan; the one in the lower hall is Kazak (Russian); the carpet in the north bedroom is a Williamsburg reproduction of a Colonial pattern woven in strips and sewn together. Most of the furniture is English or the more rare American Hepplewhite or Sheraton, predominantly of the early 1800s. The barn bell came from the Middletown (Kentucky) Tavern and was used to announce to the populace the arrival of General Lafayette in 1824. The desk in the kitchen is known to have been used by John James Audubon, the naturalist and artist. (A note taken from the desk and bearing his initials is now in the display case.)

In the doorway of the study is a Speed land grant for the very ground on which the house is built. There also are Speed pictures and letters. The old pictures of the buildings, the plot of the farm, and the blueprint of Farmington and the Jefferson plan are of interest. An important feature is a group of pictures and letters of Lincoln that recall his summer visit in 1841.

FARMINGTON is located six miles from the center of Louisville on the Bardstown Road (U.S.31E) at the intersection of the Watterson Expressway (U.S.60 -Ky.I-264). It is open on Tuesday through Saturday from 10:00 A.M. to 4:30 P.M. and on Sunday from 1:30 P.M. to 4:30 P.M. It is closed on Mondays, New Year's Day, July 4th, Thanksgiving and Christmas. Admission is seventy-five cents, children twenty-five cents.

The Gamble Mansion is, in a sense, a memorial to a way of life and a system of economy that were swept away by the Civil War. The close of the Seminole War in 1842 opened the Manatee country, in which the Gamble Mansion is located, for settlement. The mild climate and fertile soil of the area attracted men of sufficient means to engage in the cultivation of sugar cane and its manufacture into sugar. Among those planters was Major Robert Gamble.

Starting with a comparatively small acreage, Major Gamble increased his holdings from year to year until he had a plantation of 3,500 acres, of which 1,500 were under cultivation. The most modern machinery was bought in New Orleans for the sugar refinery, which consisted of three large brick buildings. Although still a bachelor, Major Gamble set his slaves to building a home in keeping with the lavish scale of his operations. Brick manufactured on the place from lime, shell, and sand was used. Some red brick was also used. The same substances were used to make the tabby with which the exterior of the building is plastered.

The mansion was built between 1845 and 1850. It is a two-story structure, ninety-three feet by forty-three feet in dimensions, with walls nearly two feet thick. Eighteen large pillars, eighteen inches in diameter and twenty-five feet high, support the roof, forming upper and lower verandas that extend across the front and two sides. In the rear is a double detached kitchen connected with the main building by the roof structure.

In 1858, due to the financial collapse of the sugar operations, the plantation was sold and leased by its new owners to W. A. Griffin. When Griffin joined the Confederate Army in 1862, Captain Archibald McNeill and his family moved into the mansion. The McNeills lived in dread of a raid by one of the numerous Federal ships blockading the west coast. On August 3, 1864, a landing party from the U. S. bark *James L. Davis* destroyed the sugar refinery, fired the buildings, and looted the mansion of all foodstuff; but they did not damage the mansion at all. For the next ten months life at the mansion was normal.

Late in May of 1865 two men drove up in a buggy and asked for lodging. One was a Captain Lesley of Tampa, who was well known in the section, and the other was introduced as a Mr. Howard. The true identity of this gentleman was revealed as Judah P. Benjamin, Secretary of State of the late Confederate States of America. Benjamin had left Richmond on April 2 with President Davis and other high Confederate officials with the intention of re-establishing the Confederate government west of the Mississippi. As the hopelessness of their cause became more and more apparent, Benjamin parted from the group and traveled south.

The Gamble Mansion proved not too safe a hiding place. Federal ships were still on the coast, anxious to capture leading Confederates, of whom Captain McNeill was one of the more prominent. During his stay Benjamin spent much of his time on the upstairs veranda scanning the river with a spyglass for gunboats. In spite of his vigilance, the Federal troops succeeded in making a surprise raid on the mansion. Benjamin and McNeill had barely time to escape through the kitchen into a thicket of scrub palmetto in the rear. Benjamin eventually reached England, where he carved out a second career for himself as a member of the English bar.

The McNeill family continued to reside in the Gamble Mansion until 1872, when it was bought at forced sale by Major George Patten for $3,000. The Patten family lived in it for a number of years but finally abandoned it rather than incur the expense of keeping it in repair. In 1925 the Judah P. Benjamin Chapter of the United Daughters of the Confederacy purchased the mansion and deeded it to the State of Florida, which had agreed to restore and preserve it as a historical memorial.

The first part of the Gamble Mansion to be built was the two-story rear building containing the kitchen, one other room on the first floor, and two rooms above it. Red brick as well as tabby fashioned into bricks were laid up, and then the walls were plastered with tabby. The main part of the house is made of red brick and the massive pillars are made of tabby bricks. Each pillar brick was wedge-shaped. When laid up, these bricks made strong cylindrical columns. Tabby is made of oyster shell lime combined with sand. Shells were used to supply the coarse aggregate.

The house has many furnishings of the period of its construction. In addition, there are some items that were in it when Mr. Benjamin was in hiding. On display is an inscribed saber that Mr. Benjamin sent to Captain McKay, one of the officers who helped him hide from the Federal troops.

THE GAMBLE MANSION

The GAMBLE MANSION is located at Ellenton, Florida, on U. S. 301 on the Manatee River. It is also designated as the Judah P. Benjamin Memorial. The Mansion is open every day except Monday. No admission is mentioned in the literature.

HAMPTON

TOWSON, MARYLAND

Hampton, one of the great postrevolutionary mansions of America, was built during the period 1783–90. For 158 years it was the home of the Ridgely family, long prominent in Maryland. Spacious in size, symmetrical in design, and conceived for gracious living, the mansion has those qualities of formal charm and elegance typical of the late Georgian style of architecture.

The roots of the Ridgely family go deep in Maryland history. Robert Ridgely migrated from England to St. Mary's County, where he resided until his death in 1681. His second son, Charles, was a planter in southern Maryland. The third Ridgely, Charles "the Merchant," moved to Baltimore County, where in April, 1745, he acquired Northhampton, a 1,500-acre tract laid out in the wilderness just fifty years before. This was the beginning of Hampton, the family estate of the Ridgelys. Within five years the initial purchase had been extended to over 7,000 acres. When iron ore deposits were found nearby, the Ridgelys bought that land also and established the Northhampton works. The iron furnace soon became one of the principal activities of the estate. During the Revolution it supplied military stores, including cannon and shot, to the patriot forces.

When the builder, Charles Ridgely, died childless in 1790, the mansion and most of the estate passed to Charles Ridgely Carnan, a nephew who then changed his name to Charles Carnan Ridgely. As governor of Maryland in 1816–19, he brought Hampton to the state of grandeur that gave it national fame. He was responsible for the formal gardens at the rear of the mansion. They consisted basically of three terraces containing two rectangular parterres each. A broad grass ramp divided the parterres on each level. These were planted in box and laid out in a formal design typical of the eighteenth century. A wide lawn separated the gardens from the mansion.

Life at Hampton attained a high degree of social elegance. The home reflected a way of life that is part of the great tradition of Maryland social hospitality. It was reported to "keep the best table in America." As many as three hundred invitations were issued for the parties at Hampton.

Many details of Hampton's construction are obscure, but it was begun in 1783. Family papers record that Jehu Howell, a local carpenter who could also have been its architect, received £3,482 13s. 6½d. for carpentry and woodwork. Many of Charles Ridgely's own ideas may have gone into Hampton's design. When completed in 1790, Hampton was one of the largest houses of its day, measuring 175 by 55 feet. Built of local stone and stuccoed, its two-and-a-half-story main section with wide porticos was set off by balanced one-story wings. Its symmetrical design presented a stately appearance, relieved by the lively skyline featuring the unusually large cupola, ornate dormers, and urnlike decorations on the roof.

The rooms in Hampton are larger than those usually found in mansions of this period and present a rather formal but comfortable appearance with their balanced design and lack of excessively ornate woodwork. Window glass and flooring are the originals. All chandeliers, except the Waterfords in the Great Hall, are also original. The shutters are on the inside of the house.

The Great Hall measures fifty-three by twenty-two feet through the north portico doorway. The Waterford chandeliers are rare, and a Kashan rug covers the floor. All the mirrors are the original ones. There is a Hepplewhite sideboard, Chippendale side chairs, and an Austrian piano. The drawing room has black and gold Empire furniture believed to have been made by Duncan Phyfe. There are unusual wall brackets of gesso. The rug is Aubusson. The music room has many examples of period furniture. The breakfront and its contents belonged to Governor Ridgely, and the harp was Eliza Ridgely's. There is an Empire sofa and a Sèvres tea set. There are excellent examples of Ridgely family china in the cabinet in the party room. The upper hall is unusual for its heavy, elaborate woodwork and its battery of doorways and closets, over which are broken pediments. The north portico room has the only complete set of Baltimore fruitwood ballroom furniture in America. Books owned by the Governor are in the bookcase. The north bedroom is associated with one of the many Hampton ghost stories. Only the Turkey carpet and chandelier are family originals. The tub and baby bath are Canton ware. Original Ridgely pieces in the master bedroom are the rug, bedspread, and the chests. The large wardrobe of ebony, satinwood, and zebrawood is a fine example of early Baltimore craftsmanship. The third floor contains ten rooms but is not open to the public.

HAMPTON can be reached from Baltimore by following Charles Street (State Route 139) or York Road (U.S. 111) north to Towson. Take Dulany Valley Road (State Route 146) past Goucher College one-half mile to Hampton Lane; the intersection is marked. Turn right at the lane that leads to the site. The mansion is open Tuesday through Saturday from 11:00 A.M. to 5:00 P.M. and on Sunday from 1:00 P.M. to 5:00 P.M. It is closed on Mondays and from January 15 to February 15. Admission is fifty cents, children twenty-five cents.

THE HOMESTEAD

FORT GEORGE ISLAND, FLORIDA

The Homestead is actually a group of houses on Fort George Island, one of the earliest sites of Florida to be occupied by the Spaniards. The McQueen House, the Kingsley House, and the brick and tabby stable make up the historic site known as The Homestead. Fort George Island was named the Island of Alimacani. It is near the mouth of the St. Johns River. The Mission of San Juan del Puerto was built on the island under the direction of Father Pareja, a leading scholar of Spain. The island was visited in 1696 by Jonathan Dickinson and Robert Barrow, the famous Quakers, when they were shipwrecked south of the island. General Oglethorpe built a fort near Mount Cornelia, maintained an outpost there, and renamed the island in honor of his king.

During the Revolutionary War Captain John McQueen of the South Carolina Navy acted as a courier for George Washington. He built The Homestead. After the war he became a Spanish subject. In 1795, as Don Juan McQueen, he was captain of the St. Marys and St. Johns Rivers for Spain. His houses and the island were later owned and occupied by Colonel John Houstoun McIntosh, director of the short-lived Territory of East Florida. His family lived on Fort George Island for ten years.

In 1817 Zephaniah Kingsley, slaver and large landowner, came into possession of Fort George Island and developed it into an extensive plantation. He built a house that is still standing and used a small house as a residence for Anna Jai, an African princess whom he married by tribal ritual. She helped manage the slaves in a competent and aloof manner. During the winter of 1868–69, John F. Rollins of Dover, New Hampshire bought Fort George Island. He occupied the Kingsley House and used the McQueen House for kitchen and dining purposes. It was he who first called the group of buildings The Homestead. Subsequently the site became a club for officers of the Army, Navy and Marine Corps. In 1951 The Homestead was purchased by the State of Florida through the cooperation of the officers and members of the club. The buildings have been repaired and painted so that they can be reviewed from the outside. However, research must be conducted before additional restoration and furnishing can proceed.

THE HOMESTEAD can be reached from Jacksonville by way of State Highway No. 105 (Hecksher Drive) turning north at the village of Fort George. It may be reached from State Highway A1A (Buccaneer Trail) near the Fort George end of the Mayport Ferry. Neither admission charges nor hours for viewing are listed in the literature.

BATH, NORTH CAROLINA

At the time of Raleigh's first expedition to Carolina in 1584, present Bath was the site of the Pomouik Indian town of Cotan. The first proprietary grant in the Pamlico River area, made in 1684, embraced the site of Bath.

David Perkins, whose farm included the site, was one of the first English settlers to arrive in this area in 1695. Perkins sold the south sixty acres of his farm to John Lawson, Joel Martin, and Simon Alderson in the fall of 1704. By an act of the Assembly on March 8, 1705, the town of Bath became the first incorporated town in North Carolina.

Three proprietary governors—Robert Daniel, Thomas Cary, and Charles Eden—resided in or near Bath and made it their seat of government. The General Assembly met in Bath from 1744 to 1752. The Lower House of the 1746 Assembly passed an act designating Bath as the first permanent capital of North Carolina. Neither the Council nor the governor approved this act, so it did not become law. Bath served as a refuge for settlers who survived the first onslaught of the Tuscarora Indian War (1711–13).

Historic Bath has become a State Historic Site. St. Thomas Church is the oldest church building in North Carolina that has been in continuous use. The St. Thomas Parish was created by the first Vestry Act of 1701. Construction of the church began in 1734 and was probably completed prior to 1740. King George II presented the church with a pair of silver candelabra. The Queen Anne Bell, housed in a small tower near the church, was presented by the Queen whose name it bears.

Glebe House was the nineteenth-century home of John F. Tompkins, agricultural reformer, a founder of the State Fair, and publisher of the *Farmer's Journal* (1852–53). The house is now the Bath Community Library.

The Palmer-Marsh House was built by Captain Michael Coutanch about 1744. Colonel Robert Palmer acquired the house in 1764. Colonel Palmer was surveyor general of the colony, served in the Assembly and on the Governor's Council, and was colonel of the Beaufort County Militia. The house remained in the Palmer family until 1796. In 1802 it was purchased by the Marsh brothers, Jonathan and Daniel G., and remained in their family for more than a century. The house is restored and open to the public for a small charge.

The Buzzard Hotel is an old inn built about 1740. It was named for its builder and operator. With the exception of St. Thomas Church, it is probably the oldest building extant in Beaufort County. It is now a private residence and not open to the public.

Bonner House is believed to have been built about 1825. In 1830 the property was sold to Joseph Bonner and remained in the family until acquired and restored as part of Historic Bath.

Harding's Landing is representative of the piers and landings that were located along Main (Water) Street. It is not a reconstruction nor a restoration.

HISTORIC BATH is located on Highway 92. It is open from Tuesday to Saturday from 10:00 A.M. to 5:00 P.M. and on Sunday from 2:00 P.M. to 5:00 P.M. It is closed on Monday. Admission is $1.00, children fifty cents.

ST. THOMAS CHURCH, BATH

HALL OF PALMER-MARCH HOUSE, BATH

HISTORIC HALIFAX

HALIFAX, NORTH CAROLINA

Colonial Halifax was an important political, social and commercial center of revolutionary and postrevolutionary eastern North Carolina. Although chartered in 1757, the Halifax region was settled as early as 1723.

In 1771 Halifax defied the royal government. When Governor Tryon called on the townspeople for help in crushing the Regulators, the townspeople refused. In 1774 the citizens of Halifax incorporated in one document a pledge of allegiance to the king and an attack on the existing methods of the Crown in its tax pro-

CONSTITUTION HOUSE, HALIFAX

cedures. This document was really a forerunner of the famous *Halifax Resolves* of 1776. In 1781 Cornwallis, en route to Yorktown, occupied and quartered his troops in Halifax. From 1777 to 1782 several sessions of the new state legislature met there, making Halifax a center of the new state government during the American Revolution. After 1783, when the General Assembly moved to Hillsboro, political activity in Halifax declined.

The *Halifax Resolves,* first formal sanction of American Independence from Great Britain, were adopted in Halifax on April 12, 1776. The Continental Congress, in session in Philadelphia, incorporated the ideas of the *Halifax Resolves* into the Declaration of Independence on July 4, 1776.

Now many of the buildings of Colonial Halifax have been restored and furnished. The Colonial Courthouse, the seat of the Provincial Congresses, and of the General Assembly in 1779, and site of the adoption of the *Halifax Resolves,* was replaced in 1840 on a new site. A stone

COLONIAL JAIL, HALIFAX

195

marks the location of the original courthouse built in 1758.

The Colonial Jail was built in 1764 and used until 1913. Scottish Loyalist prisoners were brought there under heavy guard, as were Tories and British naval prisoners. The building is now used as a museum.

Adjacent to the Jail is the old Clerk's Office, built in 1832 to replace an earlier office on the same location, which was used in 1784 as a newspaper printing office for the *Halifax Journal*.

Across the road from the Clerk's Office is the Old Cemetery and the site of the Colonial Church, which was destroyed. The Church was used by all denominations, and many early Halifax citizens are buried in the churchyard.

Constitution House was moved from its original site in 1920 and restored. It is the house in which the first North Carolina Constitution was drafted in 1776 by a nine-man committee appointed by the Provincial Congress. It is furnished in the style of the 1776 period.

The Magazine Spring was developed by the Tuscarora Indians and used by the Halifax citizents for water. Located nearby was a powder magazine that was used for many years.

The Dutch Colonial House was built about 1760 and has been restored and furnished in the prerevolutionary period style. It is a perfect example of Dutch Colonial architecture.

The Davie Home was the home of General William R. Davie (1765–1820), governor, envoy to France, Constitutional Convention member, Federalist, legislator, lawyer and a founder of the University of North Carolina. Loretta was the Halifax home of Davie from 1783 to 1805.

Next door to the Clerk's Office is the original site of the Eagle Tavern. It served as a political headquarters for members of the Provincial congresses and assemblies. It was a favorite social center, and President Washington and Lafayette were among notables entertained there. In 1845 part of the Tavern was moved four blocks south and is now a private residence.

One of the oldest lodge halls in America is the Masonic Lodge. Chartered in 1767, the building contains many of the original furnishings. The first floor of the Lodge was used as a ballroom in the 1790s and as a schoolhouse until 1829. It is closed to the public.

HISTORIC HALIFAX is located on Road 301, a main north-south highway, in Halifax, North Carolina. It is open on Sunday from 2:00 P.M. to 5:00 P.M. A receptionist is on duty at Constitution House. For the weekday schedule the visitor must contact the Halifax County Library on Main Street in Halifax. Historic Halifax is closed Saturday and Thursday afternoons.

DUTCH COLONIAL HOUSE, HALIFAX

MOORE COUNTY, NORTH CAROLINA

The House in the Horseshoe takes its name from its location in a large horseshoe bend of Deep River in northern Moore County. It is sometimes known as the Alston House, referring to an early owner, Colonel Philip Alston. During the American Revolution the house was caught within the fire of battle. Numerous bullet holes and scars still mark the walls.

After the Revolution the house became the residence of Benjamin Williams, governor of North Carolina for four terms (1799–1802), who named the plantation Retreat and converted the lands into one of North Carolina's first large cotton plantations.

On Sunday, August 5, 1781, Colonel Philip Alston, leader of a band of North Carolina Whig fighters, was camped with his men at Alston's dwelling house. Early in the morning David Fanning, a notorious Tory commander, attacked Alston's Whigs with his larger force. After a brisk two-hour battle, during which the Tories attempted to set the house on fire by rolling a cartload of burning straw against it, the Whigs sent out a white flag in the hands of Colonel Alston's wife. The Whigs were released on parole. This type of informal hit-and-run fighting between Whig and Tory bands was frequent in the North Carolina back country during the Revolution.

Alston, though a prominent and influential man from an excellent family, was a turbulent person and frequently in trouble with the law. Finally, after being implicated in a murder, he left the state. He died the next year. In 1798 Governor Williams acquired the 3,000-acre plantation. Williams had been a brave officer in the Revolution, had served in Congress, and had been a member of the first board of trustees of the University of North Carolina. He was soon to become Governor.

Williams wanted to become a planter, for after Eli Whitney's invention of the cotton gin it was profitable to grow short staple cotton in the upland South. The Horseshoe's land was excellent for this purpose. In 1801 Williams planted forty-two acres of cotton and the next year nearly two hundred acres. In 1803 he valued his plantation at $30,000. His slaves numbered between fifty and sixty.

Following William's death in 1814 the land changed ownership many times. By 1954 the dwelling house had reached a state of deterioration, and the Moore County Historical Association undertook to rescue and restore it. The house and five acres of land were acquired by the State of North Carolina to be furnished and administered by the Historical Association.

The House in the Horseshoe, built about 1700, was one of the first "big houses" in the frontier country of upland North Carolina. Its style is borrowed from the coastal lowlands. The two-story frame building has a large brick chimney on each end and a full-length shed-porch on each side. The major rooms feature good woodwork. In the "great room" are a handsome carved mantel and cornices.

THE HOUSE IN THE HORSESHOE is located on Route 421, northwest of Sanford. Visitors are requested to apply to the caretaker who lives on the site. A sign marks his house, and he is available during regular daylight hours. There is a small admission charge.

JAMESTOWN ISLAND

JAMESTOWN, VIRGINIA

The story of Jamestown began on May 13, 1607, when the first Virginia colonists, after several months of voyaging from England and a brief stay on Cape Henry, sailed up the James River and selected Jamestown Island, then a peninsula, as a place for settlement. They disembarked from their three small ships, *Susan Constant, Godspeed* and the *Discovery*. The first years at Jamestown were trying ones; sickness, hunger and inexperience were compounded by the settlement's dangerous location. Captain John Smith became the dominant personality at Jamestown, and his vigorous leadership helped keep the colony together for the first two and a half years. He departed for England in October, 1609, disabled by a gunpowder explosion.

His departure marked the beginning of the terrible "Starving Time," when nine-tenths of the colonists died. The survivors planned to leave the colony, and it was only the arrival of men and supplies and the newly appointed governor, Lord Delaware, that prevented the abandonment of Jamestown.

Gradually the colony took on a look of permanence, and plantations spread up and down the James. By 1614 the settlement boasted streets and houses. About 1611 experimentation in tobacco culture, advanced by John Rolfe, proved successful and established the economic basis on which the colony became prosperous. It was this same John Rolfe who married Pocahontas, daughter of Powhattan, in 1614 in the church at Jamestown.

-Settlements spread outward along the James, but Jamestown was the political, social, and economic center of the colony. In 1619 it was the scene of the meeting of America's first representative legislative assembly. In 1619 steps were taken to 'send women to Virginia to become wives of the settlers. The first Negroes were brought to Virginia and sold as indentured servants.

In 1622, there was a sudden uprising of the Indians, which resulted in wholesale destruction of life and property. Warned by a friendly Indian, Jamestown escaped the massacre, but for a time the whole life of the colony was threatened.

In 1624 Virginia became a royal colony. The Virginians, though loyal to the British sovereign, were increasingly conscious of their strength and jealous of their rights. In 1635 they temporarily deposed the royal governor, Sir John Harvey. Under the administration of Sir William Berkeley feeling mounted to the pitch of open rebellion. In 1676 Nathaniel Bacon the Younger emerged as the popular leader in a revolt against Berkeley. Jamestown was involved in the fighting, and for a time the governor was driven from power. Bacon's men then burned the town. Bacon died and the rebellion collapsed, leaving only a continuing spirit of resistance to tyranny.

Berkeley was replaced as governor, and Jamestown was partially rebuilt, but the town had suffered a blow from which it never recovered. In 1699 the seat of government was moved to Williamsburg, and in a few years Jamestown was practically abandoned. The town ceased to exist about the time of the American Revolution.

The first organized effort to save the Jamestown site came in 1893 when the Association for the Preservation of Virginia Antiquities acquired title to 22½ acres of land on Jamestown Island. In 1940 the Association area was designated the Jamestown National Historic Site.

Today Jamestown consists of many markers and monuments. There are the 103-foot Tercentenary Monument, the Pocahontas Monument, the House of Burgesses Monument, the Memorial Cross and others, including the ivy-covered Old Tower, the only standing ruin of seventeenth-century Jamestown. The tower is believed to have been constructed as a part of the first brick church begun in 1639. The Memorial Church adjoining the tower was erected in 1907 over the foundations of the early brick church. In the Churchyard the few remaining gravestones are witness to the antiquity of the spot.

A visit to the modern Visitor's Center, where exhibits trace the story of the life and times of Jamestown, is advisable. Many objects once used by the settlers have been unearthed from the Jamestown ruins and are on display. From the Center a walking tour extends over the townsite, along the old streets and paths to the church, the statehouse sites, and the ruins of early houses, taverns, and shops. Paintings, markers and recorded messages along the way help you imagine the life in the colony. A road loops the wildwood section of the island, and a forty-minute drive on this loop completes the Jamestown visit. Glasshouse Point, scene of the Jamestown Glassworks of 1608 and its faithfully restored counterpart, lies on the tip of the mainland. The state park, created for the 350th Jamestown anniversary, also features a reproduction of James Fort, the reconstructed ships *Susan Constant, Godspeed,* and *Discovery,* Powhatan's Indian Lodge, and other exhibits. This park has its own admissions schedule.

JAMESTOWN ISLAND is reached over the Colonial Parkway from Williamsburg, only ten miles away. Williamsburg is the nearest rail and bus terminal. The approach from the south is over State Routes 10 and 31 to the ferry over the James River. It is open daily except Christmas Day. A single admission fee of fifty cents is charged.

FREDERICKSBURG, VIRGINIA

This handsome mansion of the mid-Georgian period was built in 1752 for Betty Washington Lewis, the wife of Fielding Lewis and the sister of General George Washington. Colonel Lewis was a gentleman of substance from 1750 until his death two months after Yorktown in 1781. He was a gentleman-justice of Spotsylvania County, a leader of the Spotsylvania Militia, a surveyer, storekeeper, and plantation owner. He engaged in many enterprises with his brother-in-law, George Washington. He was appointed one of five Commissioners of Arms for the Colony of Virginia at the outbreak of the Revolution, and he manufactured arms for the Virginia Regiments at the Fredericksburg Arms Works, which he helped found and manage till his death. He also provisioned Washington's forces with salt, meat, hides and powder and built and armed three sloops for coastal defense. Since he was not paid, his acts of patriotism greatly depleted his sizable fortune.

Tradition has it that George Washington directed the execution of the exquisite ceilings and cornices throughout the lower floor. At the request of his sister he suggested the design of decoration and Aesop's Fables as the subject for the famous overmantel in the great room.

Such leaders of the Revolution as General George Washington, the Marquis de Lafayette, Count Rochambeau, General Mercer, John Paul Jones, Patrick Henry, Thomas Jefferson, and George Mason were guests at Kenmore.

The original Kenmore plantation site was 863 acres on the edge of Fredericksburg, and the tract was surveyed by the brother of the mistress of Kenmore, George Washington. The probable architect of Kenmore was John Ariss, who was responsible for many Virginia mansions. The

construction commenced in 1752 and went on for several years. The house itself is plain mid-Georgian in its exterior, gable-hipped, with four rooms on each of two floors, no dormers, and a portico on the river side. The brick exterior presents a picture of restraint and dignity. Its simplicity contrasts with the ornate interior, which has stucco duro ceilings and overmantels in the important first-floor rooms that are considered one of the finest Adam interiors anywhere as well as the earliest Adam interior in Virginia.

Kenmore originally had more than a hundred slaves and more than twenty dependent buildings. The two dependencies present today are reconstructions on old foundations. The name Kenmore was not attached to the mansion and site until about 1815, when a Scotch family, the Gordons, gave it that name. After a succession of owners Kenmore was sold in 1922 to the Kenmore Association, and the house was restored in 1930 under the direction of the lates Charles O. Cornelius of the New York Metropolitan Museum of Art. The Garden Club of Virginia restored the gardens and grounds and erected the brick wall around the property in 1932. Kenmore is an outstanding example of Tidewater Virginia architecture.

KENMORE is located on Washington Avenue in Fredericksburg, Virginia. It is open to the public every day except January 1 and 2 and December 25 and 26. It is open from 9:00 A.M. to 5:00 P.M. From November 15 to March 1 hours are 9:00 A.M. to 4:30 P.M. Adults are admitted for $1.00; children from ten to sixteen for forty-five cents, and children under ten are admitted free.

MARGARETTA MASON BROWN

FRANKFORT, KENTUCKY

This historic Georgian house was built about 1796 by John Brown, one of Kentucky's most distinguished citizens. Born in Staunton, Virginia, in 1757, the eldest son of John and Mary Preston Brown, he left Princeton when nineteen to join Washington's army. He later became aide-de-camp to General Lafayette. In 1778 he returned to Virginia to complete his education at William and Mary College and to read law under Thomas Jefferson.

In 1782 or 1783 he moved to Danville, Kentucky. During the next ten years he represented the District of Kentucky in the Virginia Senate, in the Continental Congress, and in the United States Congress. In 1792 he was elected one of the first two senators from the newly formed State of Kentucky. He served as Senator until 1805, when he retired to private life.

In 1796 Senator Brown bought about four acres of land in Frankfort and soon started the building of Liberty Hall. Bricks were made and burned at the back of the present garden, nails were made by a blacksmith nearby, and lumber was dried for two years under a huge shed. Black walnut was chosen for the interior, white and blue ash for the floors. The great brass locks for doors and glass for windows were brought from the East, probably Philadelphia.

In 1797 his former teacher and great friend, Thomas Jefferson, wrote, "Tho you thought you had made such progress in your plan that it could not be altered, yet I send you the one I mentioned as you may perhaps draw some hints from it for the improvement of yours." It is not known whether or not Senator Brown profited from any of those hints, but it seems almost certain he did not; Jefferson's letter strongly advocated a one-floor plan, but Liberty Hall is a two-story Georgian type with a colonial period portal and a Palladian window characterized by Rexford Newcomb as, "the finest—in Kentucky." The interior woodwork and architectural detail, however, show the federal influence.

In 1799 John Brown married Margaretta Mason of New York City and by 1801 had brought her and their first son, Mason, to Kentucky. In September of that year their second son, Orlando, was born at Liberty Hall.

For the remaining thirty-six years of Senator Brown's life this stately house welcomed the notables of the age. Visitors can still see the green room where President Monroe and his aides General Andrew Johnson and Major Zachary Taylor were entertained at breakfast and the cup in which Margaretta served tea to General Lafayette. Portraits by Gilbert Stuart, Chester Harding, Jonathan Trumball and Matthew Jouett still hang there. There are also many other heirlooms of Senator Brown and his descendants, who continued to occupy Liberty Hall for four generations.

The kitchen, recently restored to its original shape and function, shows where many a famous and delicious meal was prepared. The large open fireplace held a never-dying well-banked fire ready to be chunked up whenever food or hot beverage was required. There is a splendid collection of utensils, all used in this very kitchen by the Brown family. The garden is reminiscent of the lovely old gardens along the James River in Virginia. Its restoration is carried out as meticulously as that of the mansion. Four square, it boasts an abundance of authentic eighteenth-century and early nineteenth-century plants, including a fine collection of old roses, damasks, maiden's blush, souvenir de Malmaison, gallicas and many others. There are three varieties of boxwood. The first Sabbath School west of Pittsburgh was organized in this garden in 1810 by Margaretta. It met under a great old apple tree.

LIBERTY HALL is located on the corner of West Main and Wilkinson Streets in Frankfort, Kentucky. It may be visited Tuesday through Saturday from 10:00 A.M. to 5:00 P.M. and Sundays from 2:00 P.M. to 5:00 P.M. It is closed Mondays. Admission is seventy-five cents, children twenty-five cents.

HALL AND STAIRWELL, LIBERTY HALL

DRAWING ROOM FIREPLACE, LIBERTY HALL

McDOWELL HOUSE

AND APOTHECARY SHOP

DANVILLE, KENTUCKY

The McDowell House and Apothecary Shop are authentic restorations of the eighteenth-century home and shop of one of America's most famous frontier physicians and surgeons. Ephraim McDowell was born in Augusta County, Virginia, on November 11, 1771. When Ephraim was twelve years old, his father, Samuel, moved to Kentucky (then part of Virginia.)

Ephraim first studied medicine under Dr. Alexander Humphries of Staunton, Virginia. From there he went to the University of Edinburgh in 1792, where he matriculated; but he did not obtain a degree in medicine. In 1795 he returned to Kentucky and located at Danville. For the next twenty-two years he was the foremost surgeon west of the Allegheny Mountains. The only degree he held was an honorary one of M.D. conferred by the University of Maryland in 1825.

The McDowell House has nine rooms, five on the first floor and four on the second floor. In a small bedroom on the second floor it is believed that Dr. McDowell performed the first successful removal of an ovarian tumor on December 25, 1809. The room is reached by a stairway from the back of the house. It is heated by a fireplace and has a small door opening into a master bedroom that faces the street.

The house is interesting architecturally both outside and in. There is a small entrance hallway flanked by large doors opening into the rooms on each side. To the right of the front stairway with its graceful banister there is a large door leading to the back porch.

The right-hand room on the first floor is beautifully paneled and has ceiling-height recessed cabinets or bookcases on each side of the fireplace. The windows of the house are large and numerous, unusual for this period. The small panes, however, are characteristic. There are seven fireplaces, the largest that of the kitchen.

The house was acquired by the Kentucky Medical Association, dedicated and opened in 1939, and presented to the State of Kentucky. Much of the furniture of the family was restored to its original place.

The McDowell Apothecary Shop was the first drugstore west of the Alleghenies. In 1795, three years after Kentucky became the second state admitted to the union, Dr. McDowell and Dr. Adam Rankin started their practice of medicine in this two-room brick building. It was used by them and their successors as an apothecary shop continuously until 1856, when it

was purchased by the Methodist Church for use as a parsonage. Later it was a pool room, beer hall, barber shop, and restaurant.

The back room was the doctor's office, and the front room was operated as a physician-owned apothecary shop. An apprentice to the doctors prepared medicines for their patients. These old preparations included infusion of digitalis, plasters, lotions, tinctures, ointments, pills, and mixtures of rhubarb and soda, or chalk mixtures, for stomach ailments. Patent medicines from England, France, and Germany were also for sale.

The Apothecary Shop is furnished with a collection of two hundred pieces of eighteenth- and early nineteenth-century apothecary equipment and includes colorful glassware of striking period design by English, French, Scottish and American craftsmen. Seventy-six drawers are hand-lettered with gilded labels identifying the contents of the drugs popular in that period.

The McDOWELL HOUSE and APOTHE-CARY SHOP is located at 126-127 South Second Street in Danville, Kentucky. It is open Monday, Tuesday, Wednesday, and Saturday from 9:30 A.M. to 4:30 P.M., Friday from 1:00 P.M. to 4:30 P.M., and Sunday from 2:00 P.M. to 5:00 P.M. Admission is fifty cents.

MOUNT CLARE

BALTIMORE, MARYLAND

Situated on a wooded rise away from the noise and bustle of southwest Baltimore is the stately mansion Mount Clare, the only one now remaining within the city limits of Baltimore. It is the city's oldest building and only pre-revolutionary home. This distinguished plantation house has won itself a wide reputation by the beauty and balance of its Georgian lines.

Although the land for Mount Clare was acquired by Dr. Charles Carroll of Annapolis in 1732 and the house was begun in 1754, it was his son Charles Carroll, barrister, who completed it; he and his wife, Margaret Tilghman, made it a center of enlightened colonial living. Mount Clare was their summer home; race horses were bred, and the latest scientific farming and gardening were practiced. The iron furnace and flour mill also kept the owner quite busy.

When strife between the British rulers and the colonials increased, Charles Carroll played an important role on the state scene. He played a major role in drawing up Maryland's Declaration of Rights and State Constitution. He wrote to fellow members of the Council of Safety at

Annapolis advising on war preparations and reporting on conditions in Baltimore.

After the death of Charles Carroll in 1783, Mrs. Carroll lived on at Mount Clare, where her chief interests were her gardens and greenhouse, from which she supplied George Washington with rare trees and plants for Mount Vernon. Since the Carrolls had no surviving children, a nephew, James Maccubbin, inherited the place on the condition that he take the Carroll name. During his ownership the cornerstone of the Baltimore and Ohio Railroad was laid on land donated by him, and the first railroad station, Mount Clare, was built nearby. The property remained in the family until 1890. The City of Baltimore succeeded the Carroll family as owners, and since 1917 the house has been under the custody of The National Society of Colonial Dames of America in the State of Maryland.

The Palladian window above the columned entrance portico and the pilastered façade on the river side make the building noteworthy. Aside from the present two wings, which are a modern version of the former gable-roofed cottages, the house remains much as Charles Carroll left it. Many original furnishings have been returned to grace the rooms again and to recall the elegance of the eighteenth century. English plate and mahogany are now in the dining room, and in the corner cupboard gleam luster, the delicate designs of Lowestoft, and the rich blue of Nanking and Canton china.

The influence in the drawing room is French. The furniture is part of the original set ordered by the barrister for the embellishment of his home. To the right of the main entrance is the office, or study, of the barrister, which has a special entrance, a side door from the garden. The windows of the drawing and dining rooms overlook the terraces and garden to the south. A part of the lovely old patterned brick steps that led down the terrace still runs down almost to the street.

Mount Clare is in the environs of Carroll Park. It is located on Washington Boulevard, Wilkens Avenue, and Monroe Street. It can be reached by buses 3 and 51. Driving from Baltimore, go west on Franklin St. (Route 40) to Monroe St. (Route 1), then south on Monroe over a railroad bridge to Carroll Park entrance on left.

MOUNT CLARE is open daily from 11:00 A.M. to 4:30 P.M. and Sunday from 2:00 P.M. to 4:30 P.M. It closes at 4:00 P.M. from November through March. It is closed on Mondays. Admission is seventy-five cents, children under 12 twenty-five cents.

SITTING ROOM, MOUNT CLARE

OLD SALEM

MIKSCH TOBACCO SHOP, OLD SALEM

WINSTON-SALEM, NORTH CAROLINA

Old Salem is an authentic restoration of the Moravian community of Salem, a planned congregation town that fascinated George Washington when he visited it in 1791. It was founded in 1766 by ingenious Moravian artisans and craftsmen. This community, a center of crafts, was unique to the eighteenth-century South. The religious, business and social life of the town was governed by the German Protestant Moravian Church.

The influence of the Moravians' Old World background can be seen in the architecture of Old Salem. It was patterned after the central European style. Buildings were clustered around a central square; houses were built flush with the streets; and eyebrow-arched windows and tile roofs prevailed. The daily life and work of the people reflected their mid-European heritage. Salem, established two hundred miles inland, far from a navigable river or existing road, served the westward drive as a stopping point and trading center for the frontiersmen. But, like the larger coastal towns, Salem had more

to offer than simply the means of livelihood. There were teachers, preachers, and musicians. There were surgeons and apothecaries. There were craftsmen with an eye for beauty as well as usefulness. It was not until 1913 that Salem merged with Winston, its younger, more commercial neighbor to the immediate north.

Old Salem today reflects a history that has spanned seven wars and almost two centuries. Many of the buildings of the past are being used today for contemporary versions of their original purposes. Old Salem was restored by a local nonprofit group in 1950, when physical deterioration and encroaching commercialization threatened the historic site. Today, on the road to complete restoration, Old Salem offers daily tours of five exhibition buildings. The red-brick tree-shaded sidewalks and the Salem buildings greet the visitor.

Forty of the sixty buildings of the original town are still standing. Twenty-one have been restored. A wealth of original furnishings in the

219

COMMUNITY STORE, OLD SALEM

220

THE LIVING ROOM, JOHN VOGLER HOUSE, OLD SALEM

221

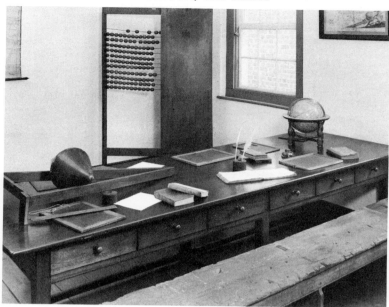

buildings have been preserved by local Moravians and historical societies. The detailed records kept by early Moravians have made it possible for restoration work to be very authentic.

During George Washington's visit in 1791 he stayed two nights at the Salem Tavern. The Tavern, with its fashionable bar, eighteenth-century-style kitchen, and comfortable rooms, is one of Old Salem's exhibit buildings. Another exhibit building is the Miksch Tobacco Shop, a gathering place for conversation and a short smoke. The shop, a small and simply constructed log building, was the first privately owned house in Salem. Built in 1771, it contained two rooms, a kitchen and a general living room. Later two bedrooms were added. The wares were displayed on shelves, tables, and chests. There were garden seeds, toys, soap, brushes, gingerbread, and candy, as well as tobacco items.

The largest and most important restoration is the newly restored Single Brothers House, where unmarried men of the community lived from the age of fourteen, when they were apprenticed to master craftsmen. The Brothers House best reflects the heart of Salem as a craft town. There artisans demonstrate the crafts of the gunsmith, tinsmith, cooper, tailor, shoemaker, potter, joiner, weaver, and dyer. A 1797 Tannenberg organ has been restored in the Saal (chapel) of the Brothers House. The organ is a living monument to the Moravians' love of music and the period of Moravian American composers now called the "Unknown Century of American Music, 1760–1860."

A silhouette machine in the John Vogler House attracted eighteenth-century visitors. It was used to make profiles of eighteenth-century guests. The house and shop of John Vogler, town jeweler, silversmith and clock repairer, is open as an example of one of the finest homes in Salem. Craft, transportation, Indian, firefighting, Revolutionary and Civil War, music, and toy exhibits are on display in the Wachovia Museum. The museum, housed in the Moravian Boys School, contains one of the largest collections of local antiquities in America.

In 1803 a small brick building was erected on the west side of Salem Square. One portion of the building housed two fire engines (the first ever used in North Carolina), the other portion was used as a meat market. The fire department consisted of the majority of residents in the village. Each was given a specific duty to perform in case of fire. The Market Fire House was reconstructed in 1955 on the original foundation of the old building.

A museum of Early Southern Decorative Arts in Old Salem contains fifteen southern period rooms and four galleries with furnishings dating from the late seventeenth century to the early nineteenth century.

OLD SALEM is located at 614 South Main Street in Winston-Salem, North Carolina. It is open weekdays from 9:30 A.M. to 4:30 P.M. and Sundays from 2:00 P.M. to 4:30 P.M. Admission to single buildings is fifty cents. A ticket for all buildings is $1.50.

225

SHADOWS-ON-THE-TECHE

NEW IBERIA, LOUISIANA

David Weeks, a wealthy Louisiana planter whose holdings included Grand Cote, Cypremort, Parc Perdu and Vermillion Bridge plantations, planned a town house for his growing family. In 1825 he chose a location central to his scattered estates, on the right bank of the Bayou Teche in the parish of St. Martin. He acquired 4½ arpents of the highest land in the town then still known variously by its Indian name of Attakapas, its Spanish name of Nova Iberia, or simply, New Town.

In 1831 he started burning bricks to build his mansion. Although each detail of the building was under his constant direction, he entrusted the erection of the mansion to James Bedell, master builder. This owner-builder collaboration was a common practice in an era of few professional architects. It was built in the prevailing classical taste, with columns and architectural features of the Tuscan order. It is a brilliant example of foreign influences that culminated in the distinctive house style of the Louisiana country.

As the house neared completion in the spring of 1834, David Weeks sailed for New Haven, Connecticut, in an effort to recover his health.

There he died and was buried, leaving his wife, Mary Clark Weeks, to manage his plantations and raise their six children. The story of the house and its family in the years until the Civil War and in the bitter years that followed is the story of the Louisiana planter class. It is the story of a life of hard work and gaiety, good times and bad, tied to the rise and fall in the prices of crops of sugar and cotton, a life of malaria and Mardi Gras, plagues of cholera and escape to resorts like Virginia Springs and Newport.

Mementos left behind tell the story of five generations of the family that always thought of the house on the Teche as the "home place." Weeks Hall, the great-grandson of its builder, returned to his native Louisiana after his service in World War I and art studies abroad to find the building and outbuildings drifting to ruin under the great oaks, in a tangle of neglected gardens. He devoted the remaining years of his life to preserving the house and recreating around it another great garden. Weeks Hall was, according to his friend Harnett Kane, the noted writer, "a man of high taste, of superb gusto and a deep love of his scene, and also of his house." He was a southern eccentric in the true sense and brought back during the twenties and thirties, the gaiety and sparkle of ante bellum hospitality. He died in 1958, and the National Trust accepted his bequest of the Shadows.

Probably few other restorations have been better documented. It was possible to verify the colors of wallpapers and fabrics in particular rooms through descriptions in family records. There were bills and receipts showing when and where certain pieces of furniture were purchased. The planting of certain trees and shrubs could be traced through journals and letters. Like any house lived in by one family over a period of years, the restored Shadows boasts a variety of furnishings including Chippendale and Hepplewhite styles of the late eighteenth century, Sheraton of the early nineteenth, and the later American Empire style. Some are Weeks heirlooms, some were purchased by Weeks Hall, and others were added by the National Trust.

The Shadows is built of soft pink brick with eight classic columns rising from the level of its garden to support the roof. In order to catch the breezes in Louisiana's humid climate, the ceilings are high, and most of the main rooms are on the second floor. Outside stairways lead from the downstairs loggias to the second-floor galleries. The only interior stairway is the "slaves" stair at the rear of the house. The chaste simplicity of its architecture, the elegant detail of its interior woodwork, the fine furniture, silver, and family portraits make the Shadows outstanding.

STAIRWAY LEADING TO UPPER GALLERY, SHADOWS-ON-THE-TECHE

SHADOWS-ON-THE-TECHE is located on Main Street and the Bayou Teche in New Iberia, Louisiana. It is open to the public daily from 9:00 A.M. to 4:30 P.M. It is closed Christmas Day. Admission to house and gardens is $1.00.

229

STANTON HALL

NATCHEZ, MISSISSIPPI

Stanton Hall stands as an imposing monument to that romantic era in the history of the Old South when cotton was king. More than five years in construction, it was built in 1851 by Frederick Stanton, one of the three brothers who came to America from Belfast, Ireland. Mr. Stanton became tremendously wealthy as a commission merchant, had plantations in Louisiana, and made money in cotton. A ship was chartered to bring materials such as carved woodwork, marble mantels, chandeliers, and other furnishings for the house from Italy and France. The gallery is laid with dark gray and white marble, the steps are granite, and the whole house is thought to be an exact replica of Mr. Stanton's ancestral home in Ireland. Today Stanton Hall is the property of the Pilgrimage Garden Club and is Official Headquarters for Tourist Information for Natchez.

The pillars in front of the house are Corinthian, the front door is two and a half inches thick, ten feet tall and four and a half feet wide. All door knobs, keyholes, and hinges are Sheffield silver. The hall is seventy-two feet long but is broken by a carved overhead arch. The carpet in the hall is unclipped Brussels. Handsome Empire tables in the hall hold two amber vases of Bohemian glass. The large pictures in the hall depict the Voyage of Life and were painted by Thomas B. Cole.

The draperies in the library are replicas of the original (brocatelle); the curtains are Brussels lace. The mirrors were brought to Natchez from France especially for the house, which is the largest in Natchez. All chandeliers are French bronze. The library chandelier has armor and weapons motifs and figures of French soldiers. As the town of Natchez was founded by the French in 1716, it is thought that Mr. Stanton

DRAWING ROOM, STANTON HALL

wanted to carry out the historic features of the town in his house ornaments. The chandeliers were originally lighted by gas. Stanton Hall had its own gas plant. The lights on the mantle were whale oil lights, and the shades are the originals.

The library and the drawing room together are seventy-two feet long, broken by an elaborately carved unsupported arch. The mantels are white Carrara marble. The motifs—cupids, fruits, and flowers—took two years to carve and are re- peated in the chandeliers of the drawing room. The rugs are Aubusson, over one hundred years old. The furniture in the room is Belter, American-made, hand-carved rosewood. The piano is a Pleyal, which won a prize in the Paris exposition. The silk for the draperies is not original but was presented to Stanton Hall by Scalamandre of New York. The table, chairs, and buffet in the dining room are Sheraton. The breakfront is Regency. The fruit set is Limoges china. The silver on the table is all

WHITE CARRARA MARBLE MANTEL IN DRAWING ROOM, STANTON HALL

Sheffield. The dining room has twin fireplaces and twin chandeliers depict the Natchez Indians, with figures of Indians on ponies, Indians shooting at eagles, oak leaves for the trees under which they held their pow-wows, and maize, the chief staple of the Indians. The vases on the dining room mantels are German Meissen. Upstairs there are six large bedrooms and a seventy-two-foot hall.

The grounds cover a city block and are shaded by twenty-two giant live oak trees. Stanton Hall is one of the 30 ante bellum houses shown on the Natchez Pilgrimage each spring.

STANTON HALL is open daily. Admission $1.00, fifty cents for children. There are accommodations for overnight guests throughout the year in the upstairs bedrooms. There is also a Carriage House Restaurant on the grounds where lunch and dinner are available.

BEDROOM, STANTON HALL

TRYON PALACE RESTORATION

NEW BERN, NORTH CAROLINA

Tryon Palace became the first fixed colonial capitol of North Carolina in 1770. Construction of the large edifice and its two wings was started in 1767 at New Bern under the supervision of John Hawks, English architect, "the first professional architect to remain in America."

Described as "the most beautiful building in the Colonial Americas," its architecture was unique in America in that it was designed as a London vincinity house "in the pure English taste," and served not only as the capitol but also as the governor's residence. The first royal governor to occupy the mansion was William Tryon, who had obtained for its erection appropriations of £15,000 from the Colonial Assembly. He was succeeded as the colony's chief executive in 1771 by Josiah Martin, who soon contracted to build on the palace grounds a smokehouse, poultry house, and dovecote.

In New Bern on August 25, 1774, met the first Provincial Convention of North Carolina, the first anywhere in America to be called and held in defiance of British orders. Governor Richard Caswell and other state officials elected under the first constitution of the independent State of North Carolina were inaugurated in the Palace on January 16, 1777. The first State General Assembly convened in this first state capitol on April 7, 1777, and other Assembly meetings were held there as late as 1794, when the state capitol was moved permanently to Raleigh.

President George Washington was entertained there at a banquet and ball on April 27, 1791, during his visit to New Bern. Many other distinguished personages were guests at the Palace.

The main building was destroyed by fire on the night of February 27, 1798. The east wing remained for some years thereafter. The west wing survived. Following extensive historical and physical research, the first phases of restoration were begun during August, 1952, on the west wing, which had been used originally for stables and carriages. About 85 percent of its bricks are original ones. Using Hawks' plans and specifications, the central buildings and the east wing have been authentically and completely reconstructed on their original foundations. Eight original red sandstone steps found on the site are utilized in the restoration. Other sandstone to match was quarried at St. Bee's in Cumberland County, England.

Two shades of the colorful paints in the interior of the main building are known to have been there originally, for they were copies from bits of plaster excavated along with thousands of other artifacts during the archaeological research.

From England came much eighteenth-century material, such as the beautiful mantels on the two chief floors in the center structure, brass locks for the mahogany doors in that building, woodwork in the parlor, library and dressing room, doorways in the dining room and upstairs drawing room, inside shutters in the council chamber, urns and stone baskets for the gardens, and the 1741 wrought-iron gate and railing at the palace approach.

Furnished throughout with genuine mid-eighteenth-century antiques, mostly predating 1770, the restoration is a mecca for connoisseurs of early furniture, silver, porcelain, pottery, pewter, paintings, prints, maps, carpets, and fireplace equipment.

The landscaped grounds feature gardens designed in the eighteenth-century manner, including a Maude Moore Latham Memorial Garden, Kellenberger Garden, Hawk's Alée with statuary, Pleached Alée, green garden, kitchen garden and work garden. There are also two "necessary houses" and five garden buildings in eighteenth-century design.

TRYON PALACE RESTORATION is located in New Bern, North Carolina on Highways 17, 55 and 70. The restoration is administered by the Tryon Palace Commission, a state agency. It is affiliated with the State Department of Archives and History. It is open to the public weekdays except Monday from 9:30 A.M. to 4:00 P.M. and Sunday from 1:30 P.M. to 4:00 P.M. There are continuous guided tours by costumed hostesses. Admission is $2.00, children $1.00.

241

When the Civil War broke out, Vance formed the "Rough and Ready Guards" and served that company as captain. Later he was named colonel of the Twenty-sixth North Carolina Regiment and was leading his own men at the Battle of Malvern Hill in Virginia when he was elected to the first of three terms as governor. After the War Vance served three full terms as United States Senator and died in Washington during his fourth term.

The Vance House is not only the birthplace of Zeb Vance but was also the home of four other outstanding members of his family: Colonel David Vance, builder of the house and an officer in the Revolution; Captain David Vance, father of the governor and an officer in the War of 1812; Dr. Robert Brank Vance, early physician, United States Congressman, and the victim of a tragic duel; and Brigadier General Robert B. Vance, elder brother of Zeb, Confederate leader, and a congressman after the War.

The Zebulon B. Vance Birthplace turns time back to the way of life led by early settlers on the North Carolina frontier. The site includes a dwelling house and six farm outbuildings. The present restoration includes the original chimney and two original fireplaces and a quantity of paneling, flooring, rafters, and foundation rock taken from the old house.

Although associated with the State's Civil War governor, the Vance House was actually erected not long after the close of the American Revolution. Three times the size of the average mountain log house, it was considered something of a showplace in its day.

The ZEBULON B. VANCE BIRTHPLACE is located in Weaverville, North Carolina on Reems Creek Road and can be reached via U.S. 19–23 (Weaverville Highway) or Blue Ridge Parkway and Ox Creek Road. It is open from Tuesday to Friday 9:00 A.M. to 5:00 P.M. and Saturday and Sunday from 2:00 P.M. to 5:00 P.M. It is closed on Monday. Admission is twenty-five cents, children ten cents.

WEAVERVILLE, NORTH CAROLINA

Once termed "the Mount Mitchell" of all of North Carolina's great men, Zebulon Baird Vance was born May 13, 1830, in a pine-log house twelve miles northeast of Asheville. From this pioneer home, surrounded by the peaks of the Blue Ridge Mountains, Zeb Vance went on to attain more high honors than any other person in the state's history—which dates back to 1585.

He was only twenty-four when he went to the North Carolina House of Commons (Representatives) and just twenty-seven when elected to the first of two terms in the United States Congress.

ZEBULON B. VANCE
BIRTHPLACE

For more than a century and a half the White House has been the home of the President of the United States. It has been the scene of many brilliant social affairs—and of sorrowful events. Like the nation itself, it bears the imprint of successive chief executives. Designed originally to avoid formal display, it has an air of dignity and charm. Now rebuilt to last for centuries, the White House retains the simplicity of its original appearance and its rich historical associations.

The cornerstone of the White House, the first public building to be erected in Washington, was laid on October 13, 1792. President Washington selected the site, and it was included on the plan of the Federal City prepared by Maj. Pierre L'Enfant, a French engineer. Plans for the house, approved by Washington, were drawn by

THE WHITE HOUSE

James Hoban, an Irish-born architect. Hoban superintended the construction of the house, its rebuilding after burning by the British forces in 1814, and the erection of the north and south porticos some years later.

In the classic style of architecture, the main façade of the White House resembles the Duke of Leinster's house in Dublin, on which the design was supposedly based. Details of other faces and the interior arrangement were probably derived from contemporary houses in England and Europe. Built of sandstone quarried on Aquia Creek, Virginia, the exterior walls were painted during the course of the construction, causing the building to be termed the White House from an early date. For many years, however, it was referred to as the President's House or President's Palace.

The White House was first occupied by President and Mrs. John Adams in November, 1800. Some of its interior had not then been completed. During President Thomas Jefferson's administration the east and west terraces were constructed. On August 24, 1814, British forces captured the city and burned the White House in retaliation for the destruction by American troops of some public buildings in Canada. Although only the partially damaged sandstone walls and interior brickwork remained when the work of reconstruction was begun in the spring of 1815, the building was ready for occupancy by President James Monroe in Decmber 1817. The south portico was built in 1824 and the large north portico over the entrance and driveway in 1829. Throughout its history the White House has kept pace with modern improvements. Spring

water was piped into the building in 1834, and gas lighting was introduced in 1848. A hot-water heating system was installed in 1853. During President Andrew Johnson's administration the east terrace was entirely removed. In 1882 the first elevator was put in, and the house was wired for electricity in 1891.

By 1902, during President Theodore Roosevelt's administration, the interior had become a conglomeration of styles and periods and the house badly needed extensive structural repairs. To correct these conditions Congress appropriated more than $500,000 to repair and refurnish the house and to construct new offices for the President. The work was finished by the end of 1902. Improvements included rebuilding and strengthening the interior, redecorating and refurnishing the entire main floor, removing the main stairway from the west end of the corridor to east of the lobby and using the space made available for enlarging the State Dining Room, providing a few rooms in the attic for servants, erecting an office building at the end of the west terrace, and reconstructing the east terrace.

A few important changes were made in the White House between 1903 and 1948. Franklin D. Roosevelt added a swimming pool, a modern electric kitchen was installed, an air raid shelter was constructed, a motion-picture theatre and a small gymnasium were added. In 1949 Congress authorized an extensive renovation of the Executive Mansion. By late 1950 old walls were supported by concrete foundations, and wooden beams and brick supporting walls of the interior were replaced with a modern steel framework. Concrete floors were laid and partition walls erected. A basement and a mezzanine were provided. In 1951 the exterior was painted white, the walls and ceilings were plastered, and the interior woodwork was installed. The White

House now has 132 rooms and twenty baths and showers. There are now fifty-four rooms and sixteen baths in the part of the house used for living quarters.

In 1961, a Fine Arts Committee on the White House was appointed by the First Lady, Mrs. John F. Kennedy, to assist in acquiring authentic historic furnishings. A special Committee for White House Paintings was later selected to obtain a permanent collection of American paintings. Notable changes in the decoration and furnishings have resulted from the work of the committees.

On the first floor the furnishings and decorations are predominately late eighteenth- and early nineteenth-century style. Furnishings of historic interest have been retained with many new additions donated by public-spirited citizens. Six classic columns separate the lobby from the main corridor. The columns and the pilasters are of varicolored Vermont marble, the floors of gray and pink Tennessee marble. Seals of the thirteen original states are carved in the marble faced opening of the stairway.

The East Room is the largest room in the White House and is used for state receptions and balls. It is decorated in white and gold. Window draperies are of lemon-gold and white silk damask. The floor is oak parquetry. The mantels are painted to resemble white marble. On the mantels are gilt candelabra of the Monroe period. On the east wall is the famous portrait of Washington by Gilbert Stuart.

The Green Room is used for informal receptions and has been almost completely restored as a Federal parlor of about the 1800 period. The walls are covered with watered moss-green silk, and the curtains are of the same material. On the darkly stained oak floor is a late eighteenth-century Axminster rug. The white marble mantel was imported from Italy in 1819 and came from the State Dining Room. The Hannibal clock and gilt vases on the mantel were purchased in France during President Monroe's administration.

The Blue Room is famous for its elliptical shape and is considered the most beautiful room in the White House. The walls are covered with striped silk in two shades of cream. Encircling the room below the cornice is a draped valance of blue trimmed with a tasseled border of purple. The curtains and valances are of the same material and design. On the oak floor is a blue Empire Savonnerie rug. The Blue Room has been redecorated to represent the period of President Monroe. On the white marble mantel are a Minerva clock and gilt candlesticks purchased in 1817 from France. The Monroe pier table was restored and placed in its original position. On it is a bust of Washington acquired by Monroe. Three of Monroe's gilt side chairs and eleven reproductions stand along the wall. The crystal chandelier resembles the one ordered by Monroe. Four bronze griffin-headed wall sconces and two large floor candelabra of the Empire period have been added.

The Red Room was completely decorated in 1961 as an American Empire parlor. The walls are magenta-red silk with a gold scroll border. Draperies and upholstery are in matching fabric. Among the donated furnishings are sofas that once belonged to Dolly Madison and Nellie Custis. An empire gilt wood chandelier hangs from the ceiling. The oak floor is covered with an antique Savonnerie rug.

The State Dining Room is exceeded in size only by the East Room. It can accomodate one hundred guests. Paneling of English oak extends from floor to ceiling. The window draperies are gold silk damask.

The Private Dining Room was refurnished in 1961 as a late eighteenth-century American dining room. It has a vaulted ceiling, white enameled wainscoting, and walls paneled in plaster. A crystal chandelier lighted with candles hangs from the ceiling.

The second floor and third floor are reserved for the Presidential family and guests. The Lincoln Bedroom, in which stands the massive eight-foot bed used by Lincoln, is restored in Victorian style. The adjoining room—the Cabinet Room from about 1865 to 1902—has been restored as a conference room. The Rose Room (Queen's Room) is to be furnished as an elegant lady's bedchamber of the early nineteenth century.

A corridor with vaulted ceiling and vari-colored Vermont marble walls gives access to the rooms on the ground floor. The china room and cloakrooms are paneled in pine from the old beams of the White House. The oval Diplomatic Reception Room was refurnished in 1960 with classical furniture and a rug with the seals of the fifty states. The library was redesigned in 1961–62 and contains a suite of rare Duncan Phyfe furniture. In 1952 the original kitchen, with the old sandstone fireplaces, was restored.

The simple dignity of the White House is enhanced by the natural beauty of its informal, carefully landscaped grounds. Flower gardens and well-kept lawns form an appropriate setting for the President's home.

THE WHITE HOUSE is located on Pennsylvania Avenue in Washington, D.C. From Tuesday through Saturdays it is open to visitors from 10:00 A.M. to 12 noon, except during the summer, when the Saturday hours are extended to 2:00 P.M. It is not open on Sundays, Mondays, and holidays. Visitors are admitted at the east entrance.

WOODLAWN PLANTATION

MOUNT VERNON, VIRGINIA

George Washington noted in his diary on February 22, 1799 (his last birthday), "Miss Custis was married at Candle light to Mr. Lawe. Lewis." There began the story of Woodlawn Plantation. It was a wedding present to Washington's nephew, Major Lewis, on his marriage to Eleanor Parke Custis, granddaughter of Martha Washington.

Washington deeded 2,000 acres of his Mount Vernon lands, which he surveyed himself. As a house site he recommended the hill overlooking Dogue Creek, the Potomac River, and the mansion at Mount Vernon: "Few better sites for a house than Gray's Hill and that range are to be found in this country or elsewhere." On his survey he marked out the hilltop as "a most beautiful place for a Gentleman's Seat."

For this hill George Washington's good friend, Dr. William Thornton, first architect of the United States Capitol, designed a mansion for the young couple. Washington did not live to see Woodlawn completed but was undoubtedly consulted about the plan.

Woodlawn is of five-part construction—a central portion with flanking wings and connecting hyphens. Beyond them, but forming part of the total composition, are a smokehouse and a dairy linked to the wings with brick walls penetrated by solid wooden doors. The bricks for the mansion were burned on the place, and local Aquia stone trims the exterior. The river façade is noteworthy for its handsome portico with columns, marble floor, and double stairway leading to the garden.

The light airy high-ceilinged rooms are enhanced by fine imported mantelpieces of carved marble, and in the lesser rooms are moulded compo ornaments in classic designs. The woodwork is handsomely detailed and well proportioned, including the winding stair with carved mahogany rail in the center hall. Original paint colors were established and replaced on the walls after careful research; the graining of doors, fashionable in that day, has been replaced.

The Lewis furnishings were mostly new and fashionable, but they also include treasured heirlooms from Mount Vernon. A harp, pianoforte, music books, needlework of rare charm and skill made by Nelly herself, and many other mementos of her happy childhood at Mount Vernon are displayed, along with memorabilia of Washington's companions-in-arms.

Of the eight children born to the Lewises, all but one and her husband predeceased Nelly. After the death of her son Lorenzo, Woodlawn was abandoned and drifted to ruin. It was sold to a group of Quakers from Philadelphia in 1846. Later owners were Paul Kester, the playwright, Miss Elizabeth Sharpe, who made important architectural repairs, and Senator and Mrs. Oscar Underwood of Alabama.

The Woodlawn Public Foundation purchased the mansion in 1948 and nine years later turned it over to the National Trust for Historic Preservation, under whose direction it was restored, furnished, and opened to the public. The Garden Club of Virginia restored the garden. From records and archaeological evidence, roads, paths and flower beds have been replaced. Two rose parterres have been copied, one from Mount Vernon, the other from Tudor Place. The circle of boxwood near the west entrance was probably slipped from bushes at Mount Vernon.

WOODLAWN PLANTATION is fourteen miles from Washington, D.C., on U. S. 1 (South), three miles from Mount Vernon, seven miles from Alexandria. It is open to the public daily from 9:30 A.M. to 4:30 P.M. It is closed Christmas Day. Admission to the house and gardens is seventy-five cents.

MUSIC ROOM, WOODLAWN PLANTATION

THE WOODROW WILSON HOUSE

WASHINGTON, D. C.

Late in 1920, as Woodrow Wilson's second term neared its end, Mrs. Wilson searched for a suitable residence. One day she visited the S Street House she later described as "an unpretentious, comfortable, dignified house, fitted to the needs of a gentleman." On December 14, Mr. Wilson presented his wife a piece of sod representing the land and a key representing the house.

Built for Henry Parker Fairbanks in 1915, the red brick house of Georgian style was designed by the late architect Waddy B. Wood. The Wilsons installed an elevator, a billiard room, and a brick garage and placed iron gates at the entrance to the drive. Stacks were built for Mr. Wilson's library of 8,000 books.

In *My Memoirs* Edith Bolling Wilson tells of their arrival in their new house: "This house, which forty-eight hours before I had seen in utter confusion, was in perfect order—curtains and pictures hung, rugs down, and flowers, flowers, flowers everywhere. Every room a bower. The place looked as if we had been there for years. Every article was in the relative position it had occupied at the White House; all the little things, and the extraordinarily large bed that had been made to order. On the wall above this bed hung a long silk banner he always valued. It had been presented to him in New York by an Italian artist during the War. The banner, about six feet in leigth, shows the Stars and Stripes flung wide to the breeze. Over the door was hung the original of the Red Cross poster called 'The Greatest Mother in the World,' and on the mantel was the empty brass shell which held the first shot fired by the American troops in the World War. And of course there were books and books."

In the library today is an extensive collection of books of the Wilsonian era, biographies of Wilson and his contemporaries, most of them presentation and incribed copies. Among them is a leather-bound set of Wilson's writings presented as a wedding gift by the Guatemalan ambassador. By the library fireplace is his leather chair inscribed in his own handwriting, "Presented to my dear wife, whose inspiration meant so much to me while I occupied this chair. Woodrow Wilson." Included in Mrs. Wilson's gifts to the Woodrow Wilson House are other furnishings identified with events in Wilson's administration, a Gobelin tapestry ("The Marriage of Psyche," made for the President and Mrs. Wilson), commemorative china and early furniture owned by the Bolling family of Virginia.

Woodrow Wilson retired in 1921 to the house on S Street. There he died three years later on February 3, 1924. Before the death in 1961 of the second Mrs. Wilson, Edith Bolling Wilson, her will had provided that this house should be presented to the American people under guardianship of the National Trust, to "preserve and maintain said premises in perpetuity as a memorial in honor of the Grantor's late husband, the Honorable Woodrow Wilson, a past president of the United States of America."

The WOODROW WILSON HOUSE is located at 2340 S. Street, N.W.. in Washington D.C. It is open to the public daily from 10:00 A.M. to 4:00 P.M. It is closed on Christmas Day. General admission is fifty cents.

DRAWING ROOM, WOODROW WILSON HOUSE

255

MIDWEST & WEST

PORTAGE, WISCONSIN

Fort Winnebago was the middle link of a chain of three forts along the Fox-Wisconsin waterway. It was begun in September, 1828, on the right bank of the Fox River, and its reservation consisted of about 4,000 acres. Three companies of the First Infantry under Major D. E. Twiggs were its first garrison.

Jefferson Davis, at that time Secretary of War, had been a young lieutenant in the first garrison. The buildings and property were ordered sold in December, 1853. The Surgeon's Quarters is the only building that now remains. It overlooks the site at the east end of the old Indian Wauona Trail where Louis Jolliet and Father Jacques Marquette left the Fox River on their famous exploring trip in 1673.

When the soldiers came to erect Fort Winnebago they found François LeRoi, operator of a portaging business, living in the house now known as the Surgeon's Quarters. He is believed to have built the house between 1819 and 1828. The United States Government bought it for the home of the medical officers. In 1834 it was remodeled and a hospital built nearby.

Surgeon Lyman Foote arrived at Fort Winnebago in 1834 and was probably the first doctor to occupy the house. After Foote's five-year tenure the Surgeon's Quarters became the home of Surgeon C. H. Laub, who remained until the last garrison left in 1845. After the evacuation of Fort Winnebago the house was occupied by a succession of families, mostly farmers. Its interior was cut up into several smaller rooms in place of the original four and the chimneys and fireplaces were removed.

In 1937 the Wisconsin Society, Daughters of the American Revolution began the restoration of the house. Plans used in the remodelling of

FORT WINNEBAGO

SITTING ROOM, FORT WINNEBAGO

1834 were furnished by the War Department and were used to restore partitions and four rooms to their original position. The locations of the fireplaces were determined by the discovery of the old foundations and footings under the floors. They were rebuilt to conform to the plan of fireplaces of the early part of the nineteenth century. The outer walls are made of pine logs hewn and squared with axes; the floor and ceiling joists are of hand-hewn tamarack poles. Much of the original flooring is still in place. The walls are plastered over the old hand-sawn and hand-tooled lathing, a portion of which has been left exposed.

The Surgeon's Quarters is furnished as a home of the Fort Winnebago period with authentic pieces used at the time as well as some that were actually in Fort Winnebago. The Surgeon's room has the old fort hospital operating table and two desks built by the soldiers. The wooden eagle that surmounted the fort gate surveys the room from one of these desks. There is also a collection of old medical books and surgeon's equipment of the time and plans and records of the fort. In other rooms there are collections of old pewter dishes and early American glassware.

The Garrison School, built in 1850 and used continuously until 1960, has been moved to the Surgeon's Quarters grounds and equipped with school furniture of the 1900 to 1915 period. A collection of school books dating from about 1840 is included.

FORT WINNEBAGO is located one mile east of Portage, on Wisconsin State Highway 33, at Fox River. It is open all year round from 9:00 A.M. to 5:00 P.M. Admission is fifty cents, children fifteen cents.

STREET OF EARLY AMERICAN SHOPS, HENRY FORD MUSEUM

LA CASA DE RANCHO LOS CERRITOS

LONG BEACH, CALIFORNIA

Jonathan Temple, an American from Massachusetts, arrived in California by way of the Hawaiian Islands in 1827; he married Rafaela, daughter of Francisco Cota, in 1830 and engaged in trade in Los Angeles from 1831. He purchased Rancho Los Cerritos (27,000 acres) in 1843. The present building was erected adjacent to an earlier adobe building, the last remains of which disappeared in the 1930s. Rancho Los Cerritos is thought to have been constructed in 1844. The architect and builder are unknown.

The building had a small part in the military exploits of the Mexican War in southern California. American troops under Commodore Stockton stopped at Temple's Ranch on the march to Los Angeles from San Pedro in August, 1846. Later in the fall of that year Benjamin David Wilson, at the time a prisoner of the Californians, was taken to Los Cerritos to serve as intermediary for peace overtures between the Californian Carillo and Stockton when the latter was once again expected to land his troops at San Pedro.

Until the 1860s cattle were the important product of the ranch. Several years of severe drought in the early 1860s destroyed the cattle industry in southern California. Temple sold Los Cerritos in 1866 (he died the same year) to Flint, Bixby and Company, a family organization whose members had come from Maine during the Gold Rush years. Sheep raising and wool production became the chief commercial interest of the ranch. Jotham Bixby, part-owner and resident manager, occupied the ranch house with his wife and children from 1866. The building was abandoned as a family residence about 1886. The ranch lands were successively subdivided; today the five-acre historic site is surrounded by the greens of the Virginia Country Club. Beyond the land is virtually completely urbanized.

The historical landmark was opened to the public in April, 1955. It is both a historic house and special library. The building and its furnishings illustrate the material conditions of rural

life during the third quarter of the nineteenth century, just prior to the great land boom of the 1880s.

The building is an adobe brick structure of Monterey colonial architectural style. It is a U-shaped structure consisting of two one-story wings, 150 feet in length, abutting against the ends of a two-story segment on the east. The courtyard within is closed on the west side by a wall pierced at the center by a carriage gateway. The formal family garden, approximately two and a half acres in size, is laid out on the east side of the building.

The interior was divided into small rooms, each approximately fifteen feet square. Two exceptions were the thirty-three-foot-long blacksmith shop and forty-seven-foot-long carriage room, later the ranch hands' dining room, in the north wing. In addition to period furnishings there are supplementary study collections: household objects including kitchen utensils and chinaware, examples of home art, toys and dolls, clothing and other items of personal adornment (primarily women's and children's), hand tools and objects of Chinese origin.

The historical library at Los Cerritos Ranch House is a branch of the Long Beach Public Library system. It houses some 2,000 titles, including books, documents and pamphlets covering the history of exploration and settlement of California during the Spanish-Mexican period and of southern California after the Mexican War and admission to statehood.

LA CASA DE RANCHO LOS CERRITOS is located at 4600 Virginia Road in Long Beach, California. It is approximately two and a half miles from Long Beach Freeway via Del Amo Boulevard off-ramp or San Diego Freeway via Long Beach Boulevard off-ramp. It is open to the public from Wednesday through Sunday from 1:00 P.M. to 5:00 P.M. It is closed on Mondays, Tuesdays, Thanksgiving, Christmas Eve, Christmas Day, and New Year's Day. There is no admission charge.

DEARBORN, MICHIGAN

Together with the Henry Ford Museum, Greenfield Village was founded in 1929 by Henry Ford. Adjacent to the Museum he placed Greenfield Village, which consists of some one hundred historic buildings transplanted from various parts of the United States to show the vast collections of Americana gathered by Mr. Ford. This collection traces three centuries of American life in the development of its arts and skills. The buildings that house part of the collection are the actual homes and shops of the famous Americans who lived and worked in them years ago. They are not reproductions. Thus the collections are shown in authentic settings and at the same time preserve structures of various types that were fast disappearing from America.

The Village is on a 260-acre site, and the nearly one hundred buildings have been restored to appear in every detail as they did so many years ago.

The Village is arranged as a typical village with the following general sections:

Crafts and Industrial

Several buildings near the main street tell the story of American crafts and industries, from trades practiced in seventeenth-century homes to the little shops that sprang up across the country following the Industrial Revolution. Craftsmen are busy daily at more than a dozen of these early trades, including the pewterer, miller, blacksmith, glassblower, tintyper, and potterer.

The Village Green

Around the green, or common, are buildings that figured prominently in the political, social and religious life of the American community. Included are the 1832 Clinton Inn, the first overnight stage stop on the route from Detroit to Chicago, and the Logan County Courthouse, where young Abraham Lincoln practiced law from 1840–47 while a circuit rider in frontier Illinois.

GREENFIELD VILLAGE

CLINTON INN, GREENFIELD VILLAGE

LOGAN COUNTY COURTHOUSE, GREENFIELD VILLAGE

HENRY FORD MUSEUM, GREENFIELD VILLAGE

Historic Houses

The homes of Greenfield Village are outstanding typical examples of architecture and furnishings from three centuries of American living. They range from simple one-room log cabins, such as the birthplace of educator William Holmes McGuffey, to the elaborate dwelling of Noah Webster, where his dictionary was completed. Other homes or birthplaces of famous Americans include those of the Wright Brothers, Henry Ford, Luther Burbank, Charles Steinmetz, and Robert Frost.

Thomas A. Edison Buildings

Several buildings in Greenfield Village trace Edison's career, beginning with the Smith Creek Depot, where young Edison was thrown from a train in 1863 for accidentally setting a baggage car afire, to the Fort Myers Laboratory in Florida, where until 1926 he experimented with the production of rubber from American plants. Nearby is a complex of buildings from Menlo Park, New Jersey, which were used by Thomas Edison during his most productive period, from 1876–86. They constitute the world's first industrial research center and brought forth the electric light, phonograph, mimeograph, telephone transmitter, radio tube, and numerous other important inventions.

Other highlights of Greenfield Village include the little shed where the first Ford was made, several early school buildings still in use, and the little paddle-wheel steamer *Suwanee,* which takes visitors around a quiet lagoon during the summer months.

In addition to the permanent collections, a number of outstanding special events are held annually. These include a national Sports Car Review, Midwest Antiques Forum, the Old Car Festival, the Midwest Muzzle Loaders Festival, and a special Christmas observance daily from early December through the holidays.

Both the Museum and the Village are open seven days a week all year. Summer hours, June 15 through Labor Day, are 9 A.M. to 6:30 P.M. Winter hours are 9 A.M. to 5 P.M. (EST). Admission to the Village is $1.40 and to the Museum, $1.40. There are special rates for families, children and educational groups. Horse-drawn carriage with a driver-guide is $1.25 additional.

WRIGHT CYCLE SHOP AND GREENFIELD VILLAGE CARRIAGE

SOME OF THE AUTHENTIC 1830 ANTIQUES USED TO REFURNISH OLD INDIAN AGENCY HOUSE

PORTAGE, WISCONSIN

In 1828 three companies of the First United States Infantry were sent to erect a fort at the Fox-Wisconsin portage. Lieutenant Jefferson Davis, just out of West Point, was sent up the Wisconsin to get out the pine logs for its construction. Fort Winnebago and its dwellings were completed "having been constructed of the green trees of the forest, cut down and sawed into boards by the hands of the soldiers."

One of the most popular officers at the Fort was the Indian agent, John H. Kinzie, who brought his bride, Juliet Magill Kinzie, there in September, 1830. They occupied one of the officer's quarters for the first months of their stay, because no house was available especially for them. Their rooms were fitted with furniture made under the direction of Lieutenant Jefferson Davis.

When the First Infantry was relieved by the Fifth Infantry, the Kinzies vacated their home in the Fort and took up their residence at the Agency quarters across the Fox River on a knoll opposite Fort Winnebago. The only building then at the Agency was an old log barracks, part of the earlier temporary quarters at the Fort, which had been removed and put up again on the Agency hill. For the convenience of the Kinzies a dairy, stable, and smokehouse were added to the barracks. They left this makeshift home to move into a newly constructed blacksmith's house. In June the government made an appropriation for an agent's house and a permanent home was erected in 1832 on the hill above the portage canal that connects Fox River with the Wisconsin. Every trace of Fort Winnebago, save the Surgeon's Quarters, has vanished,

266

OLD INDIAN AGENCY HOUSE

but the house planned in the winter of 1831–32 and finished by November, 1832, still stands. Lumber came from surrounding woods, from Green Bay and from seventy to eighty miles above on the Wisconsin River. The bricks were burned near the Wisconsin River bridge in what is now the city of Portage. Stone came from Stone Quarry Hill. The lime was burned at Pierre Pauquette's farm, called Bellefontaine, twelve miles northeast of the Fort. There were three rooms on the ground floor, one 19' x 19', one 14' x 19', one 10' x 14' and a small hall. The upper floor had a 19' x 19' room, one 14' x 19' and two 10' x 10' rooms and a small hall. The buildings were on Indian land. The shifting Indian populations in the area made Kinzie believe that his agency would be the center of the largest Indian population in the Northwest,

except Chicago, and that it would be raised from a sub-agency to a full Agency. The Kinzies lived in the Agency house until July 1, 1833. The government had refused to raise the sub-agency to a full Agency or to increase his salary. His old home, Chicago, beckoned him and he resigned and left.

After Kinzie's departure the house was used by Satterlee Clark as a trading post. When the Winnebago Indians left the region for their new reservation west of the Mississippi in the summer of 1840, the house was abandoned. Fort Winnebago was evacuated in 1845. In 1853 all of the land was sold by order of Jefferson Davis, then Secretary of War. The land on which the Agency House stood was patented to James Martin, who after three years sold to George C. Tallman. From Tallman the land became a farm, passed into the hands of the family of James B. Wells, by whom it was sold in 1878 to Edmond S. Baker, whose home it was until his death in 1928.

In 1930 an Old Indian Agency House Association was formed with a capital stock of $10,000. Shares were sold, the proceeds of which were to be used for buying and restoring the Agency House. The Association offered the project to the National Society of Colonial Dames of America in the State of Wisconsin. They accepted and proceeded with the restoration and furnishing of the house. Unfortunately most of the Kinzie possessions were destroyed in the Chicago fire after he left the Agency House, but it has been furnished with authentic antiques of the period. Some of the pieces are duplicates of the originals described in Juliet Magill Kinzie's book *Wau-Bun*, an account of her life at the Agency House.

OLD INDIAN AGENCY HOUSE is open at all seasons of the year from 9:00 A.M. to 5:00 P.M. It is off Highway 33, one and a half miles from Portage. The admission fee is fifty cents for adults and fifteen cents for children.

McLOUGHLIN HOUSE

OREGON CITY, OREGON

The McLOUGHLIN HOUSE is one of the few remaining pioneer dwellings in the region once known as the Oregon Country and which today consists of the states of Oregon, Washington, Idaho, and parts of Montana and Wyoming. The house was built in 1845–46 by Dr. John McLoughlin, chief factor and superintendent of the Columbia department of the Hudson Bay Company. The McLoughlin House was probably designed by Dr. McLoughlin himself. It is a frame building, and its architecture might best be described as a colonial style adapted to pioneer

building conditions. With the possible exception of some of the window sashes and ceilings, the materials used were most likely produced at Dr. McLoughlin's own mill at Oregon City.

Dr. McLoughlin was born of Scotch-Irish ancestry in the parish of La Rivière du Loup, below Quebec, Canada on October 19, 1784. After an informal education in medicine he entered the employment of the North West Company as a physician. He was one of the commission sent to England to arrange the union of the North West and Hudson Bay Companies in

PARLOR, McLOUGHLIN HOUSE

1821. After the reorganization he was placed in charge of the Columbia District with headquarters at Fort George and later at Fort Vancouver, which he established in 1825. As chief factor of the Hudson Bay Company, Dr. McLoughlin exerted authority second only to that of Governor George Simpson, the direct representative of the London governor and Committee of the Hudson Bay Company; he literally ruled an empire stretching from the Rocky Mountains to the Pacific Ocean and from Alaska to California.

During the period of his administration from 1824 to 1846 there were few Indian outbreaks. He not only carried out activities associated with the fur-trade industry, but he also developed agri-

culture and husbandry and opened up markets for the exportation of lumber, salmon, and flour. His kindly nature made it impossible for him to ignore the needs of American settlers who, beginning with the missionaries in 1834, came in increasing numbers to locate in the Oregon Country. He sent supplies to immigrants starving at The Dalles of the Columbia, provided passage for them in company boats, and protected them from hostile natives. He entertained the newcomers at Fort Vancouver, lent them seed grains and provisions and directed them to the fertile Willamette Valley.

In 1828 Dr. McLoughlin and Governor Simpson chose the site at the falls of the Willamette River for the construction of a saw mill. Dr. McLoughlin built several houses at the spot and blasted out a millrace. In 1842 it was surveyed and named Oregon City. With the capital of the provisional government located there, it became the chief town of the Oregon Country.

When relations between Governor Simpson and Dr. McLoughlin strained to the breaking point, Dr. McLoughlin resigned in 1845. The same year he began the construction of his home at Oregon City. He moved with his family in 1846 and occupied the house until his death on September 3, 1857.

After Dr. McLoughlin's death the house was occupied for three years by his widow and until 1880 by his daughter and son-in-law, Mr. and Mrs. Daniel Harvey. In 1903 the Oregon City Women's Lewis and Clark Club began efforts for its preservation. The house was moved from its original site at Third and Main Streets to its present site in McLoughlin Park. Since 1935 the house has been restored as nearly as possible to its original condition. Federal, state and private funds have been provided for this purpose. The house has been successfully refurnished with McLoughlin articles including his desk and bed or suitable period furniture.

The McLOUGHLIN HOUSE is located in McLoughlin Park between Seventh and Eighth Streets, less than four blocks east of Pacific Highway No. 99, Oregon City, Oregon. It is open daily except Monday from 10:00 A.M. to 5:00 P.M. during the summer and from 10:00 A.M. to 4:00 P.M. during the winter. Admission is twenty-five cents, ten cents for children.